BARCODE INSIDE BOOK

D1203605

I NEVER SANG FOR MY FATHER

BY ROBERT ANDERSON

A PLAY IN TWO ACTS

DRAMATISTS
PLAY SERVICE
INC.

Dramatists Play Service

ESTABLISHED BY MEMBERS OF THE

DRAMATISTS' GUILD OF THE AUTHORS' LEAGUE OF AMERICA

for the

HANDLING OF THE ACTING RIGHTS

OF MEMBERS' PLAYS

and

THE ENCOURAGEMENT OF THE AMERICAN THEATRE

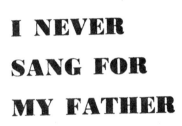

I NEVER SANG FOR MY FATHER

BY ROBERT ANDERSON

■ A PLAY IN TWO ACTS ■

DRAMATISTS
PLAY SERVICE
INC.

For

Alan Schneider

and

Gilbert Cates

I NEVER SANG FOR MY FATHER was first presented by Gilbert Cates, in association with Doris Vidor, at the Longacre Theatre, in New York City, on January 25, 1968. It was directed by Alan Schneider; scenery and lighting were by Jo Mielziner; and the costumes were by Theoni V. Aldredge. The cast, in order of appearance, was as follows:

GENE GARRISON .... Hal Holbrook

PORTER .... Earl Sydnor

TOM GARRISON .... Alan Webb

MARGARET GARRISON .... Lillian Gish

MARY .... Sloane Shelton

NURSE .... Laurinda Barrett

REVEREND PELL .... Allan Frank

MARVIN SCOTT .... Matt Crowley

WAITER .... James A. Spearman

DR. MAYBERRY .... Daniel Keyes

ALICE .... Teresa Wright

CHARACTERS
(In order of appearance)

GENE GARRISON

PORTER

TOM GARRISON

MARGARET GARRISON

MARY

NURSE (JANET HALSEY)

REVEREND PELL

WILLIAM

MARVIN SCOTT

DR. MAYBERRY

ALICE

The TIME is the Present and the Past.

The PLACE is New York City and a town in Westchester County.

I NEVER SANG FOR MY FATHER

ACT ONE

*There are no sets. A cyclorama for possible projections.
Lighting is the chief means for setting the stage.
A man comes from the rear, from the shadows. He is
Gene Garrison, age 40. He checks his watch.
A Porter passes through with a baggage cart.*

GENE. I wonder if you could help me. (*The Porter stops.*) My
Father and Mother are coming in on the Seaboard Express from
Florida. I'd like a wheel chair for my Mother if I could get one.
PORTER. You have the car number?
GENE. Yes. (*Checks slip of paper.*) 107.
PORTER. Due in at three-ten. I'll meet you on the platform.
GENE. Thank you. (*The Porter moves away and off . . . Gene
comes down and addresses the audience.*) Death ends a life, but
it does not end a relationship, which struggles on in the survivor's
mind toward some final resolution, some clear meaning, which it
perhaps never finds. (*He changes the mood.*) Pennsylvania Station, New York, a few years ago. My Mother and Father were
returning from Florida. They were both bored in Florida, but
they had been going each Winter for a number of years. If they
didn't go, my Father came down with pneumonia, and my Mother's joints stiffened cruelly with arthritis. My Mother read a
great deal, liked to play bridge and chatter and laugh gaily with
"the girls" . . . make her eyes sparkle in a way she had and
pretend that she had not had two operations for cancer, three
heart attacks, and painful arthritis. . . . She used to say, "Old
age takes courage." She had it.

My Father, though he had never been in the Service, had the
air of a retired brigadier general. He read the newspapers, all
editions, presumably to help him, make decisions about his in-

vestments. He watched Westerns on television and told anyone who would listen, the story of his life.

I loved my Mother . . . I wanted to love my Father . . . *(The lights come up on another area of the stage, where the Porter is already standing with the wheel chair and baggage cart . . . Tom Garrison is standing amidst suitcases which have been piled up on the platform. He is a handsome man, almost 80 . . . erect in his bearing, neat in his dress. He speaks distinctly, and when he is irritated, his voice takes on a hard, harsh edge. At the moment, he is irritated, slightly bewildered, on the brink of exasperation.)*

TOM. We had four bags. I don't see any of them. We had one in the compartment with us. That can't have been lost. *(He fumes for a moment. . . . As Gene watches his father for a moment, we can see in his face something of his feelings of tension. On the surface he shows great kindness and consideration for the old man . . . underneath, there is usually considerable strain.)*

GENE. Hello, Dad.

TOM. *(Beaming.)* Well, Gene, as I live and breathe. This *is* a surprise.

GENE. I wrote you I'd be here.

TOM. Did you? Well, my mind is like a sieve. *(They have shaken hands and kissed each other on the cheek.)* Am I glad to see you! They've lost all the bags.

GENE. I'm sure they're somewhere, Dad.

TOM. *(Firmly.)* No. I've looked. It's damnable!

GENE. Well, let's just take it easy. I'll handle it. *(He looks around at the luggage piled on the platform.)*

TOM. I'm confident we had four bags.

GENE. *(Quietly showing the Red-Cap.)* There's one. . . . They'll show up. Where's Mother?

TOM. What? . . . Oh, she's still on the train. Wait a minute. Are you sure that's ours? *(He looks around for bags, fussing and fuming. Shakes his head in exasperation with the world.)*

GENE. Yes, Dad. You just relax now. *(Tom is seized with a fit of coughing.)*

TOM. *(Is exasperated at the cough.)* Damn cough. You know the wind never stops blowing down there.

GENE. Don't worry about anything now, Dad. We've got a porter, and everything's under control. *(Tom snorts at this idea.*

6

Red-Cap proceeds in quiet, efficient and amused way to work the luggage.) I brought a wheel-chair for Mother.

TOM. Oh. That's very considerate of you.

GENE. I'll go get her.

TOM. I didn't hear you.

GENE. *(Raising his voice.)* I said, "I'll go get Mother."

TOM. Yes, you do that. I've got to get these damned bags straightened out. *(His rage and confusion are rising.)*

GENE. *(To Porter.)* There's one. The gray one.

TOM. That's not ours.

GENE. *(Patient but irritated.)* Yes, it is, Dad.

TOM. No. Now wait. We don't want to get the wrong bags. Mine is brown.

GENE. The old one was brown, Dad. I got you a new one this year for the trip.

TOM. *(Smiling reasonably.)* Now, Gene. I've had the bag in Florida all winter. I should know.

GENE. Dad. Please. . . . Please let me handle this.

TOM. *(Barks out an order to his son, without looking at him.)* You go get your Mother. I'll take care of the bags. *(Gene's mouth thins to a line of annoyance. He points out another bag to the Porter, who is amused . . . Gene moves with the wheel chair to another area of the stage, where his Mother, Margaret Garrison, is sitting. Margaret is waiting patiently. She is 78 . . . still a pretty woman. She has great spirit, and a smile that lights up her whole face. She is a good sport about her problems. . . . When she is put out, she says "darn" and not "damn." . . . She is devoted to her son, but she is not the possessive and smothering mother. She is wearing a white orchid on her mink stole.)*

GENE. Hello, Mother.

MARGARET. *(Her face lights up.)* Well, Gene. *(She opens her arms, but remains seated. . . . They embrace.)* Oh, my, it's good to see you. *(This with real feeling as she holds her son close to her . . .)*

GENE. *(When he draws away.)* You look wonderful.

MARGARET. What?

GENE. *(Raises his voice slightly. His Mother wears a hearing aid.)* You look wonderful.

MARGARET. *(Little-girl coy . . .)* Oh . . . a little rouge. . . .

7

This is your Easter orchid. I had them keep it in the ice box in the hotel. This is the fourth time I've worn it.

GENE. You sure get mileage out of those things.

MARGARET. (*Raising her voice slightly.*) I say it's the fourth time I've worn it. . . . Some of the other ladies had orchids for Easter, but mine was the only white one. (*She knows she is being snobbishly proud and smiles as she pokes at the bow . . .*) I was hoping it would last so you could see it.

GENE. How do you feel?

MARGARET. (*Serious . . . pouting . . .*) I'm all right, but your Father . . . did you see him out there?

GENE. Yes.

MARGARET. He's sick and he won't do anything about it.

GENE. I heard his cough.

MARGARET. It makes me so darned mad. I couldn't get him to see a doctor.

GENE. Why not?

MARGARET. Oh, he's afraid they'd send him a big bill. He says he'll see Mayberry tomorrow. . . . But I can't tell you what it's been like. You tell him. Tell him he's got to see a doctor. He's got me sick with worry. (*She starts to cry.*)

GENE. (*Comforts her.*) I'll get him to a doctor, Mother. Don't you worry.

MARGARET. He makes me so mad. He coughs all night and keeps us both awake. Poor man, he's skin and bone. . . . And he's getting so forgetful. This morning he woke up here on the train and he asked me where we were going.

GENE. Well, Mother, he's almost eighty.

MARGARET. Oh, I know. And he's a remarkable man. Stands so straight. Everyone down there always comments on how handsome your father is. . . . But I've given up. You get him to a doctor.

GENE. I've got a wheel chair for you, Mother. Save you the long walk up the ramp.

MARGARET. Oh, my precious. What would we ever do without you?

GENE. (*Is always embarrassed by these expressions of love and gratitude . . .*) Oh, you manage pretty well. (*He helps her up from the chair, and she gives him a big hug as she stands . . . and looks at him.*)

8

MARGARET. Oh, you're a sight for sore eyes.

GENE. (*Embarrassed by the intensity.*) It's good to see you.

MARGARET. (*She sits in wheel chair.*) You know, much as we appreciate your coming to meet us . . . I say, much as we appreciate your coming like this, the last thing in the world I'd want to do is take you away from your work . . .

GENE. You're not, Mother. (*Father coughs his hacking cough.*)

MARGARET. Do you hear that? I'm so worried and so darned mad. (*They arrive at the platform area.*)

TOM. Oh. Gene, this is damnable. They've lost a suitcase. We had four suitcases.

GENE. Let's see, Dad. There are four there.

TOM. Where?

GENE. Under the others. See.

TOM. That's not ours.

GENE. Yes. Your new one.

TOM. Well, I'm certainly glad you're here. My mind's like a sieve. (*Low to Gene.*) It's the confusion and worrying about your Mother. (*He shakes his head.*)

GENE. Well, everything's under control now, Dad, so let's go. We'll take a cab to my apartment, where I've got the car parked, and then I'll drive you out home.

TOM. Your Mother can't climb the stairs to your apartment.

GENE. She won't have to. We'll just change from the cab to my car.

TOM. But she might have to use the facilities.

MARGARET. No. No. I'm all right.

TOM. (*Twinkle in his eye . . . the operator.*) You know if you handle it right, you can get away with parking right out there in front of the Station. When I used to come to meet the Senator . . .

GENE. I know, but I'd prefer to do it this way. I'm not very good at that sort of thing.

TOM. Well, all right. You're the boss. It's just that you can get right on the West Side Drive.

GENE. It's easier for me to go up the Major Deegan.

TOM. Rather than the Cross County?

GENE. Yes.

TOM. I don't like to question you, old man, but I'm sure if you

9

clocked it, you'd find it shorter to go up the West Side Drive and—

MARGARET. (*Annoyed with him.*) —Father, now come on. Gene is handling this.

TOM. All right. All right. Just a suggestion.

GENE. Come on, Dad.

TOM. You go along with your Mother . . . I'll keep an eye on this luggage.

GENE. (*Trying to be patient.*) It will be all right.

TOM. (*Clenching his teeth and jutting out his jaw . . . sarcastic.*) You don't mind if I want to keep an eye on my luggage, do you? I've travelled a good deal more than you have in my day, old man, and I know what these guys will do if you let them out of your sight. (*Gene is embarrassed. The Porter smiles and starts moving off.*) Hey, not so fast there. (*And he strides after the Porter and the bags. Gene moves to the front of the stage again, as the lights dim on the retreating wheel chair and luggage, and Tom and Margaret.*)

GENE. My Father's house was in a suburb of New York City, up in Westchester County. It had been a quiet town with elms and chestnut trees, lawns and old sprawling houses with a certain nondescript elegance. My Father had been mayor of this town, a long time ago. . . . Most of the elms and chestnut trees had gone, and the only elegance left was in the pretentious names of the developments and ugly apartment houses . . . Parkview Meadows Estates . . . only there was no meadow, and no park, and no view except of the neon signs of the chain stores . . . Some old houses remained, like slightly frowzy dowagers . . . The lawns were not well kept, and the houses were not painted as often as they should have been . . . but they remained. My Father's house was one of these . . . (*Tom and Margaret have now started coming in from the back . . .*)

TOM. Just look at this town.

MARGARET. What, dear?

TOM. (*Raises his voice in irritation.*) Do you have that thing turned on?

MARGARET. Yes.

TOM. I said, "Just look at this town."

MARGARET. I know, dear, but time marches on.

TOM. Junky, ugly mess. When we came here . . .

10

MARGARET. Don't get started on that. You can't play the show over again.

TOM. I can make a comment, can't I?

MARGARET. But you always dwell on the gloomy side. Look at the good things.

TOM. Like what? . . . I'll bet you Murphy didn't bring the battery back for the Buick. I wrote him. (*He heads for the garage.*)

MARGARET. (*To Gene.*) I don't know what we're going to do about that car. Your Father shouldn't be driving any more. But they just keep renewing his license by mail . . . (*She moves stiffly, looking at her garden and trees and lawn.*) I must say, there's no place like home. Mmmmm. Just smell the grass.

GENE. (*Taking his Mother's arm.*) You all right?

MARGARET. It's just my mean old joints getting adjusted . . . I want to look at my garden . . . I think I see some crocuses . . . (*And she moves into shadows to see her garden.*)

TOM. (*Coming back.*) Well, he did bring it back.

GENE. Good.

TOM. Can't count on anyone these days. Where's your Mother?

GENE. She's walking around her garden.

TOM. What?

GENE. She's walking around her garden.

TOM. You know, Gene, I don't mean to criticize, but I noticed you're mumbling a great deal. . . . It's getting very difficult to understand you.

GENE. (*Friendly . . . hand on Dad's shoulder.*) I think you need a hearing-aid, Dad.

TOM. I can hear perfectly well if people would only enunciate. "Mr. Garrison, if you would only E-NUN-CIATE . . ." Professor Aurelio, Night School. . . . Didn't you ever have to take any public speakiing?

GENE. No, Dad.

TOM. All your education. Well . . . Where did you say your Mother was?

GENE. Walking around her garden.

TOM. (*Intense . . . he has been waiting for someone to say this to.*) I tell you, the strain has been awful.

GENE. She looks well.

TOM. I know. But you never know when she might get another

11

one of those damned seizures. (*He looks at the ground and shakes his head at the problem of it all.*)

GENE. (*Pats his Father's shoulder.*) It's rough. I know.

TOM. Well, we'll manage. She's a good soldier. But you know, she eats too fast. The doctor said she must slow down. But not your Mother. . . . Incidentally, don't forget she has a birthday coming up.

GENE. (*Who knows his Mother's birthday, and hates being reminded of it each year.*) Yes, I know.

TOM. Before you go, I want to give you some money. Go get something nice for me to give her. Handkerchiefs. You know what she likes.

GENE. (*Who has done this every Christmas and Birthday for years . . . smiles.*) All right. (*Tom coughs, deep and thick.*) We're going to have to get that cough looked into.

TOM. I fully intend to, now I'm home. But I wasn't going to let them get their hands on me down there. If you're a tourist, they just soak you.

GENE. With the problems you've had with pneumonia . . .

TOM. I can take care of myself. Don't worry about me.

GENE. Let's go see if Doctor Mayberry can see you.

TOM. First thing tomorrow.

GENE. Why not make the appointment today?

TOM. (*Irked.*) Now, look, I'm perfectly able to take care of myself.

GENE. Mother would feel better if—

TOM. (*That smile again.*) Now, Gene, don't you think I have the sense to take care of myself?

GENE. (*Smiling, but a little angry.*) Sometimes, no.

TOM. (*Looks at this, but is mollified by the smile.*) Well, I appreciate your solicitude, old man. . . . You'd better go help your Mother. . . . She's missed you a lot. . . . Why don't you stay for supper?

GENE. I was planning to take you to Schrafft's.

TOM. Hooray for our side! (*Gene starts out towards garden.*) Oh, Gene. I want to talk to you a minute. We received your four letters from California . . .

GENE. I'm sorry I didn't write more often.

TOM. Well . . . we *do* look forward to your letters. . . . But this girl . . . this woman you mentioned several times . . .

GENE. Yes?

TOM. You seemed to see a lot of her.

GENE. Yes . . . I did.

TOM. Carol's been dead now . . . what is it . . . ?

GENE. About a year.

TOM. And there's no reason why you shouldn't go out with other women . . . (*Gene just waits.*) I was in California with the Senator . . . and before that. It's a perfectly beautiful place. I can understand your enthusiasm for it. Gorgeous place.

GENE. Yes. I like it a lot.

TOM. But listen, Gene . . . (*He bites his upper lip . . . and his voice is heavy with emotion.*) If you were to go out there, I mean, to live . . . it would kill your Mother. (*He looks at his son with piercing eyes . . . tears starting. . . . This has been in the nature of a plea and an order. Gene says nothing. . . . He is angry at this order . . . that his Father would say such a thing.*) God, you know you're her whole life. (*Gene is further embarrassed and troubled by this statement of what he knows to be the truth . . . from his Father.*) Yes, you are! Oh, she likes your sister. But you . . . are . . . her . . . life!

GENE. Dad, we've always been fond of each other, but—

TOM. Just remember what I said. (*Margaret can now be heard reciting to herself . . . very emotionally . . .*)

MARGARET.

> "Loveliest of trees, the cherry now
> Is hung with bloom along the bow,
> And stands about the woodland side,
> Wearing white for Eastertide."

(*She opens her eyes.*) Oh, Gene, I've just been looking at your garden. . . . Give me a real hug . . . you haven't given me a real hug, yet. (*Gene hugs her . . . uncomfortable . . . but loving and dutiful . . . it is, after all, a small thing. Margaret looks at him . . . then kisses him on the lips. . . .*) Mmmmmmm. (*She smiles, making a playful thing of it . . .*) Oh, you're a sight for sore eyes. (*Tom has watched this, and looks significantly at Gene . . .*)

TOM. (*Moving off.*) Gene is staying for dinner. We're going to Schrafft's.

MARGARET. Oh. Can you give us all that time?

13

TOM. He said he would. Now come along. You shouldn't be standing so long. You've had a long trip. (*He goes.*)

MARGARET. He worries so about me. I suppose it is a strain, but he makes me nervous reminding me I should be sitting or lying down. . . . Oh, well. . . . (*She takes Gene's arm.*) How are you, my Precious?

GENE. Fine.

MARGARET. We haven't talked about your trip to California.

GENE. No.

MARGARET. (*Raising her voice.*) I say, we haven't talked about your trip.

GENE. We will.

MARGARET. (*Low.*) Did you speak to your Father about seeing a doctor?

GENE. He promised me tomorrow.

MARGARET. I'll believe it when I see it. He's so darned stubborn. Alice takes after him.

GENE. Oh, I got a piece of it, too.

MARGARET. (*Her tinkling laugh.*) You? You don't have a stubborn bone in your body . . . (*We fade, as they move up and into the shadows. Immediately the lights come up on another part of the stage . . . Schrafft's.*)

MARY. (*A pretty Irish waitress, is just finishing setting up her table . . .*) Well, good evening, Mr. Garrison. Welcome back.

TOM. (*The charmer.*) Greetings and salutations.

MARY. We've missed you.

TOM. It's mutual. Is this your table?

MARY. Yes.

TOM. Is there a draft here? I like to keep Mrs. Garrison out of drafts. (*He looks around for windows. Margaret and Gene come into the area. He is helping her, as she moves slowly and deliberately.*)

MARY. Good evening, Mrs. Garrison. Nice to have you back.

TOM. You remember Mary?

MARGARET. (*Polite but reserved.*) Yes. Good evening, Mary.

MARY. You're looking well, Mrs. Garrison.

MARGARET. (*As Tom holds the chair for her.*) But look at him. (*Nods at Tom.*)

MARY. We'll fatten him up.

TOM. (*Smiling, flirtatiously.*) Will you do that now? Oh, we've

14

missed you. We've had a girl down there in Florida, no sense of humor. Couldn't get a smile out of her.

MARY. Well, we'll have some jokes. Dry martini?

TOM. (*A roguish twinkle.*) You twist my arm. Six to one. (*He says this as though he were being quite a man to drink his martini this dry. Gene finds all this by-play harmless, but uncomfortable.*) You remember my son, Gene.

MARY. (*Smiles.*) Yes. (*Gene smiles back.*)

TOM. What's your pleasure, Gene . . . Dubonnet?

GENE. I'll have a martini too, please.

TOM. But not six to one.

GENE. Yes. The same.

TOM. Well!

GENE. Mother?

MARGARET. No, nothing. My joints would be stiff as a board.

TOM. (*Twinkle in his eye.*) You said you'd be stiff?

MARGARET. What?

TOM. (*Raising his voice.*) You said you'd be stiff?

MARGARET. My joints. My joints.

TOM. Oh, wouldn't want you stiff. (*He thinks he's being very funny, and tries to share his laugh with Gene, who smiles reluctantly . . . Mary goes. To Gene.*) Have I ever shown you this ring?

MARGARET. Oh, Tom, you've shown it to him a hundred times.

TOM. (*Ignoring her reminder.*) I never thought I'd wear a diamond ring, but when the Senator died, I wanted something of his. . . . Last time I had it appraised, they told me it was worth four thousand.

MARGARET. It's his favorite occupation getting that ring appraised.

TOM. (*Again ignoring her.*) Don't let anyone ever tell you it's a yellow diamond. It's a golden diamond. Of course, when I go to see a doctor, I turn it around. (*Sly smile.*)

MARGARET. (*Looking at menu.*) What are you going to have?

TOM. (*Taking out glasses.*) Now, this is my dinner, understand.

GENE. No. I invited you.

TOM. Uh-unh. You had all the expenses of coming to get us.

GENE. No, it's mine. And order what you want. Don't go read-ing down the prices first.

15

TOM. (*Smiles at the idea, though he knows he does it.*) What do you mean?

GENE. Whenever I take you out to dinner, you always read down the prices first.

MARGARET. Oh, he does that anyway.

TOM. I do not. But I think it's ridiculous to pay . . . look . . . three-seventy-five for curried shrimp.

GENE. You like shrimp. Take the shrimp.

TOM. If you'll let me pay for it.

GENE. (*Getting annoyed.*) No! Now, come on.

TOM. Look, I appreciate it, Gene . . . but on what you make . . .

GENE. I can afford it. Now let's not argue.

MARGARET. Tell me, lovey, do you get paid your full salary on your Sabbatical?

GENE. No. Fifty percent.

TOM. Well, then, look . . .

MARGARET. Now, Father, he wants to pay. Let him pay. (*They consult their menus.*) Incidentally, Tom, you should go over and say hello to Bert Edwards. Gene and I stopped on our way in.

TOM. Why?

MARGARET. While we were gone, he lost his wife.

TOM. Where'd he lose her?

MARGARET. Tom!

TOM. Just trying to get a rise.

MARGARET. And Mrs. Bernard. She looks terrible.

TOM. Always did.

MARGARET. She lost her husband six months ago. She told me, just before we left for Florida, "I hope I go soon."

TOM. Why are you so morbid tonight?

MARGARET. I'm not morbid. They're just there. . . . We really should see them, have them in.

TOM. Phooey! Who needs them?

MARGARET. Oh, Tom! . . . I can't have anyone in. Your Father won't play bridge or do anything. He just wants to watch Westerns or tell the story of his life.

TOM. Now, wait a minute.

MARGARET. I can't invite people to come over to watch Westerns or to listen to you go on and on. You embarrass me so. You insist on going into the most gruesome details of your life.

16

TOM. People seem to be interested.

MARGARET. What?

TOM. Have you got that turned up?

MARGARET. Yes. (*She adjusts the volume.*)

TOM. I said, "They seem to be interested." (*He tries to take Gene in on an exasperated shaking of the head, but Gene looks the other way.*)

MARGARET. I admit it's a remarkable story, your life. But there are other things to talk about. People want to talk about art or music or books.

TOM. Well, let them.

MARGARET. He keeps going over and over the old times. Other people have had miserable childhoods, and they don't keep going over and over them. . . . That story of your Mother's funeral. And you say I'm morbid.

GENE. What was that? I don't remember that.

MARGARET. Oh, don't get him started.

TOM. Your Mother wants me to play cards with a lot of women who just want to gossip and chatter about styles. That's why I won't play.

MARGARET. You won't play because you can't follow the play of the cards any more.

TOM. I beg to disagree.

GENE. Please. . . . Don't fight . . . don't fight. (*He's said this in a mock serious sing-song.*)

MARGARET. He kept telling everyone how he wouldn't allow his Father to come to his Mother's funeral.

TOM. (*Defensively angry.*) Are you implying that I should have let him?

MARGARET. I'm not saying—

TOM. —He'd run out on us when we were kids, and I told him—

MARGARET. —I'm not saying you were wrong. You're so defensive about it. I'm saying you're wrong to keep bringing it up.

TOM. You brought it up this time.

MARGARET. Well, I'm sorry. Imagine going around telling everyone he shoved his Father off the funeral coach. (*She is consulting the menu.*)

TOM. And I'd do it again. I was only ten, but I'd do it again. . . . We hadn't seen him in over a year, living, the four of us, in a miserable two-room tenement, and suddenly he shows up weeping and begging, and drunk, as usual. And I shoved him off! (*He almost relives it.*) I never saw him again till some years later when he was dying in Bellevue . . . of drink. (*The hatred and anger are held in, but barely.*)

MARGARET. (*Has been studying the menu.*) What looks good to you?

TOM. (*A hard sharp edge to his voice.*) I have not finished! I went down to see him, to ask him if he wanted anything. He said he wanted an orange. I sent him in a half dozen oranges. I would have sent more, except I knew he was dying and there was no point in just giving a lot of oranges to the nurses. The next morning he died. (*There is a silence for a moment, while Gene and Margaret look at the menu, and Tom grips and ungrips his hand in memory of his hatred for his Father.*)

MARGARET. (*Gently.*) Look at your menu now, Father. What are you going to eat?

TOM. I don't feel like anything. I have no appetite. (*He lights a cigarette.*)

MARGARET. (*To Gene.*) This is the way it's been.

GENE. He'll see a doctor tomorrow. Don't get upset. (*Mary arrives with the martinis . . .*)

TOM. Ah, here we are.

MARY. Six to one. (*She puts martini in front of him.*)

TOM. Damn it. (*He fishes out the lemon peel.*)

MARY. But you always ask for lemon peel.

TOM. (*Demonstrating.*) Twisted over it, not dumped in it. It's all right. It's all right. (*Irish accent.*) Well, to your smilin' Irish eyes.

MARY. He hasn't changed, has he?

TOM. What county are you from, did you say?

MARY. Armagh.

TOM. I knew there was something I liked about you. That's where my people came from. To County Armagh. (*He drinks.*) Do you have any burnt ice-cream tonight?

MARY. Ah, you.

TOM. (*Smiling.*) No, I mean it. (*To Gene.*) They have burnt ice cream here.

MARY. I'll be back. (*And she goes away. Margaret sits embar-*

rassed and piqued by this kind of flirtation which has gone on all their lives.)

TOM. (*The sport, to Gene.*) I like to get a rise out of them. If they kid with me, I give them a good tip. If they don't, a straight ten percent. (*He draws a line on the tablecloth to emphasize this. He looks at Margaret.*) What's the matter?

MARGARET. If you want to make a fool of yourself, go right ahead. (*Tom is angry, hurt and exasperated. He looks at her, and then tries to include Gene, to make him share his anger. But Gene looks away and to the menu. Tom stares at his glass, and his jaw muscles start to work. The scene dims in the Schrafft's area, and Gene moves from the table, to another side of the stage.*)

GENE. We hurried through the last part of our dinner. . . . My Father ate only his dessert . . . Burnt Almond ice cream . . . we hurried through to rush home to one of my Father's rituals. . . . The television Western. . . . He would sit in front of them hour after hour . . . falling asleep in one and waking up in the middle of the next one . . . never knowing the difference. . . . When my Father fell in love with a program, it was forever. . . . All during my childhood we ate our dinner to the accompaniment of Lowell Thomas and Amos and Andy. . . . If anyone dared to talk, Father would storm away from the table and have his dinner served at the radio . . . I say, we rushed away from Schrafft's. . . . Actually my Father rushed . . . we just lived down the street . . . I walked my Mother home very slowly . . . stopping every fifty yards or so . . . (*Margaret has joined Gene, and taken his arm.*)

MARGARET. I don't know how he can sit through hour after hour of those Westerns.

GENE. I think he always wished he'd been a cowboy. "Take 'em out and shoot 'em!"

MARGARET. He won't listen to the things I want to hear. Down in Florida there's only one TV in the lounge, and he rode herd on it. And then he'd fall asleep in three minutes. . . . Still, he's a remarkable man.

GENE. Good old Mom.

MARGARET. Well, he is. Not many boys have fathers they could be as proud of.

GENE. I know that, Mom . . . I'm very . . . proud of him.

19

MARGARET. (*She catches his tone.*) Everything he's done, he's done for his family. (*Gene just looks at her . . . smiling.*) So he didn't dance with me at parties. (*She smiles at Gene.*) You took care of that.

GENE. You were just a great dancer, Mother.

MARGARET. I was a terrible dancer. You just couldn't stand seeing me sitting alone at a table at the Club while your Father was . . . (*She stops . . . realizing she's about to make Gene's point.*)

GENE. . . . off dancing with various other people . . . table-hopping, or playing poker with the boys in the locker room.

MARGARET. What a shame that children can't see their parents when they're young and courting, and in love. All they see them being is tolerant, sympathetic, forbearing, and devoted. All the qualities that are so unimportant to passionate young people.

TOM. (*Appears.*) Gene . . . Gene . . . Come watch this one. This is a real shoot-'em-up.

GENE. In a minute, Dad.

MARGARET. Gene, I want to talk to you.

GENE. You should be in bed. You've had a big day. (*They move to another part of the stage.*)

MARGARET. I took another nitro. And I've had something on my mind for a long time now. You remember you gave me that heart-shaped pillow when I was in the hospital once, when you were a boy? (*She sits on chaise longue.*)

GENE. Yes.

MARGARET. Fidget used to curl up here. (*Indicates crook in her leg.*) And you'd sit over there, and we'd listen to the Metropolitan Opera Broadcasts. (*Gene is made uncomfortable by this attempt to evoke another time, another kind of relationship, but he doesn't show it.*)

GENE. Yes. I remember.

MARGARET. You'd dress up in costumes and act in front of that mirror. I remember you were marvelous as D'Artagnan in The Three Musketeers. (*For the fun of it, a 40-year-old man, he assumes the duelling stance, and thrusts at his image in an imaginary mirror. Gene sits on a footstool and watches her adjust herself in her chaise. . . . After a moment.*) Tell me about California.

GENE. (*A little taken by surprise. Here is the subject.*) I loved it.

20

MARGARET. And the girl . . . the woman with the children? The doctor? (*Gene doesn't say anything. He frowns, wondering what to say . . .*) You love her too, don't you?

GENE. I think so.

MARGARET. I know when Carol died, you said you'd never marry again. . . . But I hoped you would. I know it's hard, but I think Carol would have wanted you to.

GENE. I don't know.

MARGARET. (*Fidgets a moment from embarrassment, then:*) I know it's not a Mother's place to pry and talk about these things. . . . But I've been worried about you, I mean, you're a man . . . and . . . well . . . sex.

GENE. (*Smiles.*) I'm . . . all right.

MARGARET. You mean you've been . . . communicating?

GENE. (*Broad smile.*) Yes. . . . I've been . . . communicating.

MARGARET. You don't mind my talking about that, do you?

GENE. (*Amused and a little embarrassed.*) No.

MARGARET. I'll never understand your generation, I guess. I'm glad I didn't have to face all . . . well, all that, in my day. People simply waited. And I'm not so sure we weren't right.

GENE. (*Not wanting to go into it.*) Well . . .

MARGARET. Too late for me to worry about that now. Though sometimes I wish I'd known more . . . understood more . . . (*Stops . . . embarrassed. Gene is sad and uncomfortable that his 78-year-old Mother would seem to want to talk to someone at last about her unsatisfactory sex life. . . . The moment passes.*) Gene, your Sabbatical is over soon, isn't it?

GENE. A few more months.

MARGARET. I think you want to move to California and get a job teaching there and marry this woman.

GENE. (*After a moment.*) Yes. I think I do. I wasn't sure while I was there . . . I suddenly felt I should get away and think. But when I walked into my old apartment, with all Carol's things there . . .

MARGARET. I think it would be the best thing in the world for you to get away, to marry this girl.

GENE. (*Touched . . . very simply.*) Thanks.

MARGARET. A new place, a new wife, a new life. I would feel just terrible if you didn't go because of me. There are still planes, trains and telephones, and Alice comes from Chicago once or twice a year and brings the children.

GENE. Thanks, Mother. You've always made things very easy. I think you'll like Peggy.

MARGARET. I'm sure I will. You have good taste in women. And they have good taste when they like you.

GENE. I'm not so sure. I never really knew if I made Carol happy . . . If I did make her happy, I wish she'd let me know it.

MARGARET. I guess a lot of us forget to say "thank you" until it's too late . . . (*She takes his hand and smiles at him.*) Thank you. . . . You have such nice hands. I've always loved your hands. . . . You've been so good to me, Gene, so considerate. Perhaps I've let you be too considerate. But it was your nature, and your Father just withdrew behind his paper and his investments and his golf. And our interests seem to go together. You liked to sing, and I played the piano, oh, miserably, but I played. (*She strokes his hand.*) I tried not to be one of those possessive mothers, Gene. If I did things wrong, I just did the best I knew how.

GENE. You did everything just fine. (*He pats his Mother's hand before he draws his own away.*)

MARGARET. And your Father has done the best he knew how.

GENE. Yes. (*This is her old song. She knows that Gene knows it's probably true, but he gets no satisfaction from the knowledge.*)

MARGARET. Of course you know your Father will object to your going away.

GENE. He already has. He said it would kill you.

MARGARET. How sad. Why can't he say it would kill him? He doesn't think it would hold you or mean anything to you. (*She shakes her head.*) He dotes on your letters down there. Reads them and re-reads them. Tells everyone what a fine relationship he has with you. "My door is always open. . . ." "Anything he wants, he can have. . . ." "We have always had each other's confidence. . . ." (*Gene smiles at this, sadly shakes his head . . .*) Well, you go to California. Your Father and I can take care of each other. I'll remember where he put his checkbook, and he'll make the beds, which is the only thing I'm really not supposed to do. And, for your information, I have my Old

22

Lady's Home all picked out. . . . That's what I want, so I won't be a burden to any of you.

GENE. You a burden!

MARGARET. (*Wisely.*) Oh, yes. . . . Now don't mention this business to your Father tonight. He's not well, and it's been such a nice day. In the next few days, I'll talk to him, tell him it's important for you to—

GENE. No, I'll do it. (*He kisses her on the cheek.*)

MARGARET. Good night, my precious.

GENE. Where would you like to celebrate your birthday?

MARGARET. Oh, lovey, you've already given me so much time. Just call me on the phone.

GENE. No. . . . We can at least have dinner . . . I'll make some plans.

MARGARET. Gene, if your Father gives you money to buy his present for me, please no more handkerchiefs.

GENE. He always says "handkerchiefs."

MARGARET. I know, but I've got dozens and dozens from my past birthdays and Christmases.

GENE. What would you like?

MARGARET. Get me some perfume. . . . You choose the kind, except I don't like Lily of the Valley . . . or Gardenia.

GENE. You're a hard woman to please. . . . Good night. . . . You look great.

MARGARET. Oh, a little rouge and lipstick. . . . Thanks for coming to meet us. . . . Tell your Father I've gone to bed, and don't let him keep you there to all hours watching television . . . (*Calling after him.*) I don't like Carnation either . . . (*Gene waves back, affectionately . . . and moves away . . . as the lights dim on Margaret's area . . . Gene moves . . . then stands and looks at the back of his Father's chair . . . as the TV sounds come up . . . and lights come on in that area . . . Gene moves to his Father's chair . . . gently touches his arm . . . while turning the knob of the TV volume.*)

TOM. (*Stirring.*) What? . . . What? (*He comes to slowly . . . shakes his head, and looks at Gene . . . bewildered.*)

GENE. (*Gently.*) I'm going now, Dad.

TOM. Oh, so soon?

GENE. (*Controls his irritation. . . . This has always been his*

Father's response . . . no matter how long he has been with him.) Yes. I have to go.

TOM. Where's your Mother?

GENE. She's upstairs. She's fine. (*Tom starts to cough.*) You see about that in the morning, Dad.

TOM. (*Getting up . . . steadying himself.*) I fully intend to. I would have done it down there, but I wasn't going to be charged outrageous prices. (*Glance at TV screen.*) Oh, this is a good one. Why don't you just stay for this show?

GENE. (*The anger building.*) No, Dad. I've got to run along.

TOM. Well, all right. We see so little of you.

GENE. I'm up at least once a week, Dad.

TOM. Oh, I'm not complaining. (*But he is.*) There just doesn't seem to be any time. . . . And when you are here, your Mother's doing all the talking. . . . The way she interrupts. She just doesn't listen. And I say, "Margaret, please." . . . But she goes right on . . . Well, all's lost, all's spent, when we our desires get without content . . . 'tis better to be that which we destroy, than by destruction dwell with doubtful joy.

GENE. (*Is always puzzled by his Father's frequent use of this quotation. . . . It never is immediately appropriate, but it indicates such unhappiness that it is sad and touching to him . . .*) We'll get a chance to talk, Dad. (*Moves towards porch.*)

TOM. I can't tell you what a comfort it is knowing you are just down in the city. Don't know what we'd do without you. . . . No hat or coat?

GENE. No.

TOM. It's still chilly. You should be careful.

GENE. (*Kissing his Father on the cheek.*) Good night, Dad. I'll call you tomorrow to see if you've gone to the doctor's.

TOM. Well, I may and I may not. I've looked after myself pretty well for almost 80 years. I guess I can judge if I need to see the doctor or not.

GENE. (*Angry.*) Look, Dad . . .

TOM. Seventy years ago when I was a snot-nosed kid up in Harlem, a doctor looked at me and said if I were careful, I'd live to be twenty. That's what I think about doctors. Ten dollars to look at your tongue. Phooey! Out! Who needs them?

GENE. Look, Dad, you're worrying Mother to death with that cough.

24

TOM. All right, all right. I'll go. I'll be a good soldier. . . . You're coming up for your Mother's Birthday, aren't you?

GENE. Yes.

TOM. And don't forget, Mother's Day is coming up.

GENE. Well . . .

TOM. Why don't we make reservations at that restaurant in Connecticut where you took us last Mother's Day?

GENE. We'll see.

TOM. It will be my party. . . . And, Gene, remember what I said about California!

GENE. (*Straining to get away from all the encirclements.*) Good night, Dad. (*He moves off.*)

TOM. Drive carefully. I noticed you were inclined to push it up there a little. (*Gene burns.*) Make a full stop going out the driveway, then turn right.

GENE. (*Angry, moves further down.*) Yes, Dad.

TOM. (*Calling after him.*) Traffic is terrible out there now. Used to be a quiet little street. Take your first left, and your second right.

GENE. (*Has driven this route for many years.*) Yes.

TOM. Then left under the bridge. It's a little tricky down there. (*When he gets no response, he calls.*) Gene?

GENE. (*In a sudden outburst.*) I've driven this road for twenty years, for Christ's sake! (*He is immediately sorry, turns away from his Father's direction.*)

TOM. Just trying to be helpful. (*The lights fade on Father, as he goes back into the house . . . Gene is now downstage. . . .*)

GENE. Take your first left and your second right. . . . Then turn left under the bridge. . . . But do not go as far as California . . . because it would kill your Mother . . . I hated him for that, for sending up warning flares that if I left, it would not be with his blessing, but with a curse . . . as he had banished my sister Alice, years ago, for marrying a Jew . . . and the scene so terrified me at fourteen, I was sick. . . . He knew his man . . . that part of me at least . . . a gentleman who gave way at intersections. . . . And yet . . . when I looked at those two old people, almost totally dependent on me for their happiness. . . . This is the way the world ends, all right . . . (*A phone rings. . . . Light bumps on Tom holding phone.*)

TOM. I was downstairs in the kitchen, and suddenly I heard

your Mother scream . . . "Tom! Tom!" . . . I ran up the stairs . . . (*He is seized with a fit of coughing.*) I ran up the stairs, and there she was stretched out on the floor of the bedroom . . . "Nitro . . . nitro." . . . That's all she could say. You know we have nitroglycerine all over the house. (*A nurse comes to Tom as lights come up and leads him into hospital waiting room area . . . Gene joins them.*)

GENE. Dad. (*He shakes his hand and kisses him on the cheek.*)

TOM. Am I glad to see you! Have you seen your Mother?

GENE. Yes. She's sleeping. (*Tom starts to cough.*) That doesn't sound any better.

TOM. Well, I've had a shot. After your Mother got settled over here, the doctor took me to his office and gave me a shot. I *would* have gone down there in Florida, you know, but . . . well . . . (*Shakes his head.*) I just don't know. I was in the kitchen getting breakfast. . . . You know I've been getting the breakfasts, when suddenly I heard her scream, "Tom. Tom." I went running up the stairs, and there she was stretched out on the floor. She'd had an attack. "Nitro," she whispered. We've got it all over the house, you know. She'd had attacks before, but I knew at once that this was something more . . . I gave her the pills and called the doctor . . . "This is an emergency. Come quick." . . . The doctor came, gave her a shot . . . and called the ambulance . . . and here we are. (*He shakes his head, partly in sorrow, but also partly in exasperation that such a thing could happen.*) She had a good time in Florida. I don't understand it. She ate too fast, you know. And the doctor had said she should do everything more slowly . . .

GENE. There's no explaining these things, Dad.

TOM. I suppose I could have seen more of her down there. But she just wanted to play bridge, and I didn't play, because the ladies just chattered all the time about styles and shops. . . . And I met some very interesting people. Oh, some of them were bores and just wanted to tell you the story of their life. But there were others. . . . You know I met a man from Waterbury, Connecticut, used to know Helen Moffett . . . I've told you about Helen Moffett, haven't I? . . . When I was a kid, when the clouds were low and dark, my grandfather'd take me up there sometimes on Sundays . . . a city slum kid in that lovely country. . . . And Helen and I . . . oh . . . it never amounted to much. We'd go to church, and then we'd take a walk and sit in a hammock or under an apple tree. I think she liked that. But I didn't have any money, and I couldn't go up there often. Her mother didn't like me. . . . "The young man will end up the same way as his Father." . . . And that scared her off . . . This man in Florida, I've got his name somewhere . . . (*He fishes out a notebook and starts to go through it.*) He said Helen had never married. . . . Said she'd been in love as a kid . . . and had never married. (*Tears come to his eyes.*) Well, I can't find it. No matter. (*Gene doesn't know what to say. He is touched by this naked and unconscious revelation of an early and deeply meaningful love . . . but it seems so incongruous under the circumstances . . .*) Someday we might drive out there and look him up . . . Helen's dead now, but it's nice country. I was a kid with nothing . . . living with my grandfather. . . . Maybe if she hadn't been so far away. . . . Well, that's water over the dam.

GENE. (*After long pause, touches his Father.*) Yes.

TOM. (*Just sits for a few moments . . . then seems to come back to the present . . . takes out his watch.*) You know, I'd like to make a suggestion.

GENE. What, Dad?

TOM. If we move right along, we might be able to make the Rotary Club for dinner. (*Gene frowns in bewilderment.*) I've been away for three months. They don't like that very much if you're absent too often. They drop you or fine you. How about it? (*He asks this with a cocked head and a twinkle in his eye . . .*)

GENE. I thought we might eat something around here in the hospital.

TOM. I had lunch in the coffee shop downstairs, and it's terrible. . . . It will only take a little longer. . . . We won't stay for the speeches, though sometimes they're very good . . . very funny. We'll just say "hello" to the fellows and get back. . . . Your Mother's sleeping now. That's what they want her to do.

GENE. (*Bewildered by this, but doesn't want to get into an argument.*) Let's drop by and see Mother first.

TOM. They want her to rest. We'd only disturb her.

GENE. All right.

TOM. (*As they turn to go, he puts his arm around Gene's shoul-*

27

der . . .) I don't know what I'd do without you, old man. (*As the lights shift, and Tom and Gene head away, we move to the Rotary gathering . . . held in the Grill Room of one of the local country-clubs. . . . Possibly a piano is heard off-stage, playing old-fashioned singing-type songs [badly]. . . . A tinkle of glasses . . . hum of men talking and laughing . . . This area is presumably an outer hallway or locker-room, where the men leave their coats. . . . A man enters, wearing a large name button, and carrying a glass . . . This is the minister, Doctor Pell, a straightforward, middle-aged man.*)

DR. PELL. Hello, Tom, good to see you back.

TOM. (*His face lights up in a special "greeting the fellows" type grin . . .*) Hello, Sam.

DR. PELL. Did you have a good trip?

TOM. All except for that damned wind down there. . . . Oooops. Excuse my French, Sam. . . . You know my son, Gene . . . Reverend Pell.

DR. PELL. Yes, of course. Hello, Gene. (*They shake hands.*)

TOM. Gene was a Marine. (*Gene frowns . . .*) You were a Marine, weren't you, Sam?

DR. PELL. No. Navy.

TOM. Well, same thing.

DR. PELL. Don't say that to a Marine. (*Gene and Dr. Pell smile.*)

TOM. Gene saw the flag go up on Iwo.

GENE. (*Embarrassed by all this inappropriate line.*) Let's order a drink, Dad.

TOM. Sam, I've been wanting to talk to you. . . . Now is not the appropriate time, but some bozo has been crowding into our pew at church. . . . You know Margaret and I sit up close because she doesn't hear very well. . . . Well, this guy has been there in our pew. I've given him a pretty sharp look several times, but it doesn't seem to faze him. Now, I don't want to seem unreasonable, but there is a whole church for him to sit in.

DR. PELL. Well, we'll see what we can do, Tom.

TOM. (*Calling to bartender.*) A martini, George . . . six to one. (*To Gene.*) Dubonnet?

GENE. A martini.

TOM. Six to one?

GENE. Yes. Only make mine vodka.

28

TOM. Vodka? . . . Out! Phooey!

DR. PELL. What have you got against vodka, Tom?

TOM. It's Russian, isn't it? . . . However, I don't want to influence you. . . . Make his vodka. Six to one, now! These fellows like to charge you extra for a six to one, and then they don't give you all the gin you've got coming to you.

DR. PELL. I hope you don't drink many of those, Tom, six-to-one.

TOM. My grandmother used to give me, every morning before I went to school, when I was knee high to a grasshopper . . . she used to give me a jigger of gin with a piece of garlic in it . . . to keep away colds. I wonder what the teacher thought. . . . Phew. I must have stunk to high Heaven. . . . She used to put a camphor ball in my necktie too. . . . That was for colds, too, I think. . . . But they were good people. They just didn't know any better. That's my Grandfather and my Grandmother . . . I lived with them for a while when I was a little shaver, because my Father . . . well, that's another story . . . but my Grandfather—

DR. PELL. (*Hand on Tom's arm.*) —I don't mean to run out on you, Tom, but I was on my way to the little boy's room . . . I'll catch up with you later.

TOM. Go ahead. We don't want an accident.

DR. PELL. (*As he is going . . . to Gene.*) You got a great Dad there. (*And he disappears.*)

TOM. I don't really know these fellows any more. . . . (*Indicating people off.*) All new faces. . . . Most of them are bores. All they want to do is tell you the story of their lives. . . . But sometimes you hear some good jokes. . . . Now, here's someone I know. . . . Hello, Marvin.

MARVIN. (*A man about 65.*) Hello, Tom. Good to see you back.

TOM. You remember my son, Gene.

MARVIN. Yes. Hello.

GENE. Hello, Mr. Scott.

MARVIN. Well, young feller . . . you look great . . . (*To Tom.*)

TOM. Do I? Well, thank you . . .

MARVIN. How's Margaret? (*Tom goes very dramatic . . .*

29

pauses for a moment and bites his lip . . . Marvin looks at Gene.)

GENE. Mother's . . .

TOM. Margaret's in an oxygen tent in the hospital.

MARVIN. *(Surprised that Tom is here . . . looks at Gene . . . then to Tom.)* I'm terribly sorry to hear that, Tom.

TOM. Heart. *(He shakes his head and starts to get emotional.)*

GENE. *(Embarrassed.)* We're just going to grab a bite and get back. Mother's sleeping, and if we were there, she'd want to talk.

MARVIN. I'm sorry to hear that, Tom. . . . When did it happen?

TOM. *(Striving for control . . . his emotion is as much anger that it could happen . . . and self-pity . . . as anything else . . .)* This morning . . . I was in the kitchen, getting something for Margaret, when suddenly I heard her scream . . . "Tom . . . Tom . . ." and I ran upstairs . . . and there she was stretched out on the bedroom floor . . . "Nitro . . . nitro" . . . she said. . . . We have nitroglycerine all over the house, you know . . . since her last two attacks. . . . So, I get her the nitro and call the doctor . . . and now she's in an oxygen tent in the hospital . . . *(The bell starts to ring to call them to table . . .)*

MARVIN. Well, I hope everything's all right . . . Tom . . .

GENE. Thank you . . .

TOM. What happened to those martinis? . . . We've got to go into dinner and we haven't gotten them yet.

GENE. We can take them to the table with us.

TOM. I have to drink mine before I eat anything. . . . It brings up the gas. . . . Where the Hell are they? *(And he heads off. . . .)*

MARVIN. *(To Gene.)* He's quite a fella . . . *(And they move off . . . as Rotarians start singing to the tune of Auld Lang Syne . . . "We're awfully glad you're here . . . etc. . . ." As the lights fade on this group . . . they come up on the hospital bed . . . and Margaret . . . the Nurse is sitting there . . . reading her movie magazine . . . the oxygen tent has been moved away. As the lights come up on the hospital room . . . Tom and Gene enter quietly . . . cautiously . . . The Nurse gets up . . . Gene approaches the bed . . .)*

GENE. *(Whispers to Nurse.)* Anything?

30

NURSE. The doctor was just here. He said things looked much better.

TOM. (*Too loud.*) Hooray for our side.

MARGARET. (*Stirs.*) Hm. . . . What? (*She looks around.*)

GENE. Hello, Mother.

MARGARET. Oh, Gene. (*She reaches as though to touch him. . . .*) Look where I ended up.

GENE. The doctor says you're better tonight.

MARGARET. (*Her eyes flashing.*) You know how this happened, don't you? Why it happened? (*She nods her head in the direction of Tom . . . who is at the foot of the bed chatting with the Nurse.*)

GENE. (*Quieting.*) Now, Mother. Take it easy. He's seen the doctor. He's had his shot.

MARGARET. Well!

GENE. You should be sleeping.

MARGARET. That's all I've been doing. (*She takes his hand.*) It makes me so mad. I was feeling so well. All the ladies down in Florida said I'd never looked so well.

GENE. You've had these before, Mother. Easy does it.

MARGARET. He's seen the doctor for himself?

GENE. Yes. Just a bad cold. He's had a shot.

MARGARET. Why wouldn't he have that down there?

GENE. Mother, we'll have to go if you talk like this, because you should be resting.

TOM. (*Leaving the Nurse . . . cheerful.*) Well, how goes it?

MARGARET. How do I know?

TOM. (*Takes her hand and smiles.*) You look better.

MARGARET. You know I came without anything. I've still got my stockings on.

TOM. (*Kidding . . . very gentle.*) Well, it all happened pretty quick, my darling.

MARGARET. I'll need some things.

TOM. Your wish is our command.

GENE. I'll write it down. But don't talk too much.

MARGARET. Toothbrush . . . some night clothes. I'm still in my slip . . . a hairbrush.

TOM. We'll collect some things.

MARGARET. (*Joshing.*) Oh, you. You wouldn't know what to bring. Gene, you look around.

GENE. Yes. Now, take it easy.

MARGARET. I hate being seen this way.

TOM. We think you look beautiful.

GENE. Mother, we're just going to sit here now, because you're talking too much. . . . You're being a bad girl. (*Margaret makes a child-like face at him, puckering her lips and wrinkling her nose. . . . She reaches out for his hand . . .*) Those are lovely flowers Alice sent. She knows your favorites . . . I called her . . . I'll keep in touch with her. She said she'd come on, but I said I didn't think she had to.

MARGARET. Did you have any dinner?

TOM. We went to Rotary. Everyone asked for you.

MARGARET. That's nice. (*The Doctor comes into the room . . . in the shadows of the entrance . . .*)

GENE. (*Spotting him . . . going to him.*) Hello, Dr. Mayberry.

DR. MAYBERRY. Hello, Gene. How are you?

GENE. (*Trying to catch him before he enters the room entirely.*) I'd like to—

DR. MAYBERRY. (*Pleasant and hearty.*) We can talk right here. She seems to be coming along very well.

GENE. Good.

TOM. That's wonderful news.

DR. MAYBERRY. (*Kidding her.*) She's tough. (*Margaret smiles and makes a face at him.*) We won't know the extent of it until we're able to take a cardiogram tomorrow. It was nothing to toss off lightly . . . but it looks good now.

GENE. Well . . . thank you. (*Tom coughs.*) What about that?

DR. MAYBERRY. He'll be all right. Just a deep cough. He'll get another shot tomorrow.

GENE. (*Low.*) You don't think we should . . . stay around . . .

DR. MAYBERRY. I wouldn't say so. And she should rest.

GENE. Thanks, Doctor. (*He shakes hands.*)

DR. MAYBERRY. Do I have your number in New York? I'll keep in touch with you. Your Dad's a little vague about things. (*Gene jots number on paper.*) Good night, Mrs. Garrison. I'm going to kick your family out now so that you can get some rest.

MARGARET. (*Smiles and makes a small wave of the fingers.*) Take care of Tom.

DR. MAYBERRY. He's going to be fine. (*To Tom.*) Drop into the office for another shot tomorrow.

TOM. (Kidding.) Will you ask that girl of yours to be a little more considerate next time?

DR. MAYBERRY. Oh, you can take it.

TOM. Oh, I'm a good soldier. But, wow! (He indicates a sore rump.)

DR. MAYBERRY. Good night. (He waves his hand and disappears.)

GENE. We'll run along now, Mother. (She reaches her hand out.)

MARGARET. My precious.

GENE. (Leans down and kisses her hand.) Good night. Sleep well.

TOM. Well, my dearest, remember what we used to say to the children. "When you wake up, may your cheeks be as red as roses and your eyes as bright as diamonds."

MARGARET. (Pouts . . . half kidding.) Just you take care of yourself. . . . And get the laundry ready for Annie tomorrow.

TOM. (With a flourish.) Your wish is my command.

MARGARET. I put your dirty shirts from Florida in the hamper in the guest bathroom, and my things are—

GENE. (Trying to stop her talking.) —We'll find them.

MARGARET. (To Gene.) Thanks for coming. Don't bother to come tomorrow. Father will keep in touch with you.

GENE. We'll see. . . . Good night. (He stops at the door for a little wave. . . . She wiggles her fingers in a small motion. The lights dim on the hospital scene as Tom and Gene move away. . . .)

TOM. Well, that's good news.

GENE. Yes.

TOM. She looks a lot better than when they brought her in here this morning, I can tell you that.

GENE. She looked pretty good.

TOM. She's a good soldier. . . . Do you remember what she asked us to bring her? . . . My mind is like a sieve.

GENE. I'll come along and get the bag ready and round up the laundry.

TOM. We should get the laundry ready tonight because Annie arrives at eight, sharp, and she starts getting paid the minute she enters the door. . . . But we could leave the bag till morning.

33

GENE. (*Uneasy.*) I've got an early appointment at college to-morrow, Dad. I'll have to run along after we have a nightcap.

TOM. Oh, I thought you might spend the night.

GENE. I . . . uh . . . I've got an early appointment at college tomorrow.

TOM. I thought you were on your Sabbatical.

GENE. I am. . . . But I arranged a meeting with someone there, Dad.

TOM. You could stay and still make it.

GENE. It's very early, Dad.

TOM. We've got an alarm. Alarm clocks all over the house.

GENE. I want to change before the appointment. . . . Shirt . . .

TOM. I've got plenty of shirts . . . underwear . . . socks . . .

GENE. (*More uncomfortable.*) I don't wear your sizes, Dad.

TOM. I could get you up earlier, then. I don't sleep beyond five these days.

GENE. (*Tense.*) No, Dad . . . I just . . . No. I'll come by and—

TOM. There may be something good on television . . . Wednesday night. I think there is . . .

GENE. . . . We'll watch a little television, Dad . . . and have some drinks. . . . But then I'll have to go.

TOM. (*After a moment.*) All right, old man. (*Gene instinctively reaches out to touch his Father's arm, to soften the rejection—they look at each other a moment, then Tom drifts off into the dark, as Gene moves directly downstage . . .*)

GENE. I sat with my Father, much longer than I meant to. . . . Because I knew I should stay the night. But . . . I couldn't. . . . We watched television. He slept on and off . . . and I went home. . . . The next morning, around nine-thirty, my Mother died . . . (*Gene turns and walks u., as the lights dim.*)

END OF ACT ONE

ACT TWO

Gene and Dr. Mayberry enter from the rear. Gene is carrying a small overnight case containing his Mother's things.

GENE. Thank you for all you've done for her over the years. It's been a great comfort to her, to us all.

DR. MAYBERRY. I was very fond of her.

GENE. She was terribly worried about my Father's health. Yesterday she said to me, "You know what put me here."

DR. MAYBERRY. Well, Gene, I think that's a little too harsh. She's been living on borrowed time for quite a while, you know.

GENE. Yes. . . . Where's Dad?

DR. MAYBERRY. He's gone along to the undertaker's. He wanted to wait for you, but since we couldn't reach you this morning, he went along. We sent your Mother's nurse to be with him till you arrived.

GENE. Thank you.

DR. MAYBERRY. He's all right. You know, Gene, old people live with death. He's been prepared for this for years. It may in some way be a relief. He's taken wonderful care of her.

GENE. Yes, he has.

DR. MAYBERRY. Alice will be coming on, I suppose.

GENE. I've called her.

DR. MAYBERRY. He shouldn't be staying in that house alone. (*Gene nods.*) Now, you have the suitcase and the envelope with your Mother's things?

GENE. Yes. I think she should have her wedding ring.

DR. MAYBERRY. Maybe you ought to check with your Father . . .

GENE. No. . . . Will you . . . ? (*Hands ring to Doctor . . . and moves away. . . . The lights come up on the undertaker's office . . . Tom and the Nurse are there . . .*)

TOM. I find that constant wind down there very annoying. Every

35

year I think it's going to be different, but it isn't. You get a little overheated in the sun, and when you walk out from behind some shelter, it knifes into you.

GENE. (*Has stood looking at his Father for a moment. He now comes to him with tenderness, to share the experience.*) Dad.

TOM. (*Looks up in the middle of his story.*) Oh, Gene. (*He gets up shakily. They embrace. Gene pats him on the back. Tom steps away and shakes his head. His mouth contorts, showing emotion and anger that this should have happened. . . . He looks at the floor in moments like this.*)

NURSE. We've given him a little sedative.

TOM. (*Looks up.*) What?

NURSE. I said we'd given you a little sedative.

TOM. (*At once the charmer.*) Oh, yes. . . . This lovely lady has taken wonderful care of me.

GENE. (*To Nurse.*) Thank you.

TOM. It turns out she's been to Florida, very near to where we go.

GENE. (*A little surprised at this casual conversation . . . but playing along.*) Oh, really?

TOM. I was telling her it was too bad we didn't have the pleasure of meeting her down there. But she goes in the summer. . . . Isn't it terribly hot down there in the summer?

NURSE. The Trade Winds are always blowing.

TOM. Oh, yes, those damnable winds. . . . We wanted this young man to come join us there, but he went to California instead. (*To Gene.*) You'll have to come down to Florida sometime. See what lovely girls you'd meet there!

GENE. (*Baffled and annoyed by this chatter but passes it off.*) I will.

TOM. What was your name again? My mind's like a sieve.

NURSE. Halsey.

TOM. (*Courtly.*) Miss Halsey. . . . My son, Gene.

GENE. How do you do?

TOM. Miss Halsey and I are on rather intimate terms. . . . She . . . uh . . . gave me my shot.

GENE. Good.

TOM. (*To Nurse.*) I had this terrible cough down there. . . . The winds. But I'll be all right. Don't worry about me. If I can get some regular exercise . . . get over to the Club. (*For a mo-

ment, they just all sit there. Obviously there is to be no sharing of the experience of the Mother's death . . .)

GENE. I called Alice . . .

TOM. Oh. Thank you. (*To Nurse.*) Alice was my daughter . . . She . . . uh . . . lives in Chicago.

NURSE. (*Shaking his hand, kindly*) Goodbye, Mr. Garrison.

TOM. Oh, are you going?

NURSE. Yes. Take good care of yourself.

TOM. Oh, well . . . thank you very much, my dear. You've been very kind.

GENE. Thank you. (*Nurse exits.*)

MR. SCOTT. (*Entering with some forms and papers.*) Now, Tom, all we have to do is— (*Looks up from papers and sees Gene.*) Oh, hello, Gene.

GENE. Mr. Scott.

MR. SCOTT. I'm terribly sorry.

GENE. Thank you.

MR. SCOTT. Now, the burial is to be where, Tom? (*Throughout he is simple, considerate and decent.*)

TOM. The Upper Burial Ground. I've got the deed at home in my file cabinet, if I can ever find it. For years I've meant to clean out that file cabinet . . . but I'll find it.

MR. SCOTT. (*To Gene.*) Will you see that I get it? At least the number of the Plot?

GENE. It's 542.

MR. SCOTT. You're sure of that?

GENE. My wife was buried there last year.

TOM. (*Suddenly remembering.*) That's right. (*He reaches out and puts his hand on Gene's arm . . . implying that they have something to share. Gene doesn't really want to share his Father's kind of emotionalism.*)

MR. SCOTT. (*Has been making notes.*) We'll need some clothes . . . uh . . .

GENE. (*Quickly.*) Yes, all right. I'll take care of that.

MR. SCOTT. Do you want the casket open or closed while she's resting here? (*There is a pause.*)

GENE. Dad?

TOM. What was that?

GENE. Do you want the casket open or closed?

FATHER. Oh . . . open, I think. (*Gene would have preferred it closed, but . . .*)

MR. SCOTT. Now . . . an obituary. Perhaps you would like to prepare something, Tom.

TOM. Yes. Well . . . Gene. Gene was very close to his Mother. (*Mr. Scott looks at Gene.*)

GENE. Yes, I'll work something up.

MR. SCOTT. If you could, by this afternoon so that it would catch the—

TOM. —She was my inspiration. When I met her, the clouds hung low and dark. I was going to Night School, studying shorthand and typing and *elocution* . . . and working in a lumber yard in the daytime . . . wearing a cutaway coat, if you please, someone at the church had given me . . . I was making a home for my brother and sister. . . . My Mother had died, and my Father had deserted us . . . (*He has gone hard on his Father . . . and stops a moment . . .*) "He did not know the meaning of the word 'quit.'" They said that some years ago when The Schoolboys of Old Harlem gave me an award. You were there, Gene?

GENE. Yes.

TOM. "Obstructions, yes. But go through them or over them, but never around them." Teddy Roosevelt said that, I took it down in shorthand for practice. . . . Early in life I developed a will of iron . . . (*You can feel the iron the way he says it.*) Any young man in this country, who has a sound mind and a sound body, who will set himself an objective, can achieve anything he wants within reason." (*He has said all this firmly, as though lecturing or giving a speech. . . . He now looks at his cigarette.*) Ugh . . . filthy habit. Twenty years ago a doctor told me to give these things up, and I did. But when things pile up. . . . Well. . . . All's lost, all's spent, when we our desires get without content . . . (*He looks around . . . there is a pause.*)

GENE. I'll write something.

TOM. About what?

GENE. Mother. For an obituary.

TOM. Oh, yes, you do that. He's the lit'ry member of the family. . . . You'll use the church, won't you? . . . Not the Chapel. I

38

imagine there'll be hundreds of people there . . . Garden Club
. . . Woman's Club . . . Mother's Club.

MR. SCOTT. I'm sure that Reverend Pell will use whichever you
want. . . . (*He shuffles some papers.*) Now, Tom, the only thing
that's left is the most difficult. We have to choose a coffin . . .

TOM. Do we have to do that now?

MR. SCOTT. It's easier now, Tom . . . to get it over with.

TOM. (*Firm.*) I want the best. . . . That's one thing. I want
the best.

MR. SCOTT. (*Moves across the stage . . . with Tom and
Gene . . .*) There are many kinds.

TOM. (*As he takes a few steps, he takes Gene's arm.*) I don't
know what I'd do without this young fellow. (*This kind of word-
bribery disturbs Gene. . . . In the coffin area. . . . Overhead
lights suddenly come on. . . . Shafts of light in the darkness.
. . . Tom claps his hand to his forehead.*) Do I have to look at
all these?

MR. SCOTT. (*Gently.*) It's the only way, Tom. The best way
is to just let you wander around alone and look at them. . . .
The prices are all marked on the cards inside the caskets . . .
(*He lifts an imaginary card.*)

TOM. (*Puts on his glasses to look.*) Nine hundred? For the
casket?

MR. SCOTT. That includes everything, Tom. All our services,
and one car for the mourners. Other cars are extra.

TOM. (*To Gene . . . who is standing back . . .*) Well, we'll
have your car, so we shouldn't need another. . . . Anybody else
wants to come, let them drive their own car. (*Looks back at
caskets.*) Oh, dear. . . . Gene! (*Gene comes alongside. . . . He
is tender and considerate to the part of his Father who is going
through a difficult time . . . though irritated by the part that
has always angered him. They walk silently among the caskets
for a few moments . . . Tom lifts a price tag and looks at
it . . .*) Two thousand! (*He taps a casket.*) What are these made
of?

MR. SCOTT. (*Coming forward.*) They vary, Tom. . . . Steel,
bronze . . . wood.

TOM. What accounts for the variation in prices?

MR. SCOTT. Material . . . workmanship. . . . The finish inside. You see, this is all silk.

TOM. I suppose the metal stands up best.

MR. SCOTT. Well, yes. (*Tom shakes his head, confused.*) Of course the casket does not go directly into the ground. We first sink a concrete outer vault.

TOM. Oh?

MR. SCOTT. That prevents seepage, et cetera . . .

TOM. That's included in the price?

MR. SCOTT. Yes. (*Tom walks on . . . Gene stays in shadows . . .*)

TOM. How long do any of these stand up? (*Gene closes his eyes . . .*)

MR. SCOTT. It's hard to say, Tom. . . . It depends on the location. . . . Trees, roots, and so on.

TOM. I suppose these metal ones are all welded at the seams?

MR. SCOTT. Oh, yes.

TOM. Our plot up there is on a small slope. I suppose that's not so good for wear . . . I didn't think of that when I bought it. . . . And the trees looked so lovely . . . I never thought . . .

MR. SCOTT. (*Gently.*) I don't think it makes that much difference, Tom.

TOM. (*Moves along . . . stops.*) For a child?

MR. SCOTT. Yes.

TOM. (*Shakes his head . . . moved.*) My Mother would have fit in that. . . . She was a little bit of a thing. . . . Died when I was ten. (*Tears come to his eyes.*) I don't remember much about her funeral except my Father. . . . He'd run out on us, but he came back when she died . . . and I wouldn't let him come to the cemetery. . . . (*He gets angry all over again . . . then . . .*) Oh, well . . . water over the dam. But this made me think of her . . . a little bit of a thing. (*Gene is touched by his Father's memory of his own Mother . . . but still upset at this supermarket type of shopping.*) Five hundred. . . . What do you think of this one, Gene? (*Gene comes up . . .*) I like the color of the silk. . . . Did you say that was silk or satin?

MR. SCOTT. Silk.

GENE. I don't think it makes much difference, Dad. Whatever you think.

TOM. I mean they all go into this concrete business. . . . (*He senses some disapproval on Gene's part and moves on . . . ad-*

justs his glasses.) This one is eight hundred. I don't see the difference. Marvin, what's the difference?

MR. SCOTT. It's mostly finish and workmanship. They're both steel.

TOM. I don't like the browns or blacks. . . . Gray seems less sombre. Don't you agree, Gene?

GENE. Yes, I do.

TOM. Eight hundred. . . . Is there a tax, Marvin? (*Gene turns away.*)

MR. SCOTT. That includes the tax, Tom.

TOM. All right. Let's settle for that, then, and get out of here. (*He shivers.*)

MR. SCOTT. Fine. (*To Gene.*) And you'll send some clothes over?

GENE. Yes. (*Gene bobs his head up and down . . . annoyed with the details . . . though Mr. Scott has been considerate and discreet . . .*)

MR. SCOTT. I'd estimate that Mrs. Garrison should be . . . that is, if people want to come to pay their respects . . . about noon tomorrow.

GENE. All right.

MR. SCOTT. Would you like to see where Mrs. Garrison will be resting?

GENE. (*Definite.*) No, thank you . . . I think we'll be moving along.

MR. SCOTT. I assume your sister Alice will be coming on?

GENE. She arrives this evening. . . . (*He looks around for his Father . . . and sees him standing in front of the child's coffin . . . staring at it. . . . He goes over to his Father and takes him gently by the arm.*) Shall we go, Dad?

TOM. (*Nods his head . . . far away.*) She was just a little bit of a thing . . . (*And they start moving out of the room . . . as the lights dim out. . . . As the lights come up again on another part of the stage, Alice, Gene's older sister, is coming on. She is in her early forties, attractive, brisk, realistic, unsentimental.*)

ALICE. Shouldn't we be getting home to Dad?

GENE. (*Carrying two highballs . . . he is blowing off steam.*) I suppose so, but I'm not ready to go home yet. . . . Let's sit over here, where we can get away from the noise at the bar.

ALICE. You've had quite a day.

GENE. I'm sorry for blowing off, but damn it, Alice, our Mother died this morning, and I've wanted to talk about her, but she hasn't been mentioned except as "my inspiration," which is his cue to start the story of his life.

ALICE. I'm sorry you've had to take it all alone.

GENE. Well, I'm glad as Hell you're here, and I'm glad of the chance to get out of the house to come to meet you . . . I'm so tired of hearing about "when the clouds hung low and dark" . . . I'm so tired of people coming up to me and saying, "Your Dad's a remarkable man." Nobody talks about Mother. Just, "He's a remarkable man." Christ, you'd think he died! . . . I want to say to them, "My Mother was a remarkable woman. . . . You don't know my Father. You only know the man in the newspapers. He's a selfish bastard who's lived on the edge of exasperation all his life. You don't know the bite of his sarcasm. The night he banished my sister for marrying a Jew did not get into the papers."

ALICE. Shhh . . .

GENE. What a night that was! Mother running from the room sobbing. You shouting at him and storming out, and the two of us, Father and Son . . . left to finish dinner, in silence. Afterwards, I threw up.

ALICE. I shouted, and you threw up. That was pretty much the pattern.

GENE. I know I'm being unfair. But I'm in the mood to be unfair. I've wanted to turn to him all day and say, "For Christ's sake, will you for once shut up about your miserable childhood and say something about Mother?" . . . (*A little ashamed of his outburst.*) But I can't say that. He's an old man and my Father, and his wife has died, and he may be experiencing something, somewhere, I know nothing about. (*He shakes his head, for going on like this.*) I'm sorry.

ALICE. It's all right.

GENE. No. . . . (*He touches her arm, smiles.*) Mother loved your flowers.

ALICE. I've felt guilty about Mother, all the way coming here. I should have seen her more, invited her more often, brought the kids more often. Instead, I sent flowers.

GENE. I guess that's an inevitable feeling when a person dies. I feel the same way.

42

ALICE. But you were so good to her. You made her life.

GENE. (*Has always hated that phrase. . . . Slowly, quietly.*) A son is not supposed to make his Mother's life. . . . Oh, I loved Mother. You know that. But to be depended on to make her life. . . . Dad says, he boasts, he never knew the meaning of the word "quit." Well, he quit on her all right. And I . . . I was just there. (*Alice looks at this sudden revelation of his feelings, his resentment that he was left to save his Mother from loneliness and unhappiness . . .*) Still, wait till you see him. There's something that comes through . . . the old Tiger. Something that reaches you and makes you want to cry. . . . He'll probably be asleep when we get home, in front of television. And you'll see. The Old Man . . . the Father. But then he wakes up and becomes Tom Garrison, and I'm in trouble. . . . Last night he asked me to stay with him, and I didn't . . . I couldn't. I'm ashamed of that now.

ALICE. (*Touched by the complexity of Gene's feelings, looks at him a long moment, then . . .*) Have you called California?

GENE. (*Frowns . . . a problem.*) No. (*He takes a drink, wanting to avoid the subject.*)

ALICE. I suppose we have enough problems for the next few days, but . . .

GENE. After?

ALICE. Yes. We'll have to start thinking about Dad, about what we're going to do.

GENE. (*Nods his head.*) I don't know. (*They look at each other a moment, then . . .*) Well, let's go home. (*He rises.*) Thanks for listening to all this, Alice. . . . You had to pay good money to get someone to listen to you. I appreciate it. (*He smiles.*) I thought I wanted to talk to you about Mother, but all I've done is talk about him, just like the others.

ALICE. We'll talk. There'll be time. (*And they leave. . . . The lights dim out on the "Bar" area and come up on the "Home" area. . . . Tom is asleep . . . his head forward . . . his glasses on . . . some legal papers in his lap. . . . Quiet like this, he is a touching picture of old age. . . . The strong face . . . the good but gnarled hands. . . . He is the symbol of FATHER. . . . The television is on. As Gene and Alice come in, they pause and look. They are impressed by the sad dignity. . . . Finally, Gene*)

43

approaches and gently puts his hand on his Father's arm . . .
turns down television.)

GENE. Dad?

TOM. *(Barely stirs . . .)* Hm?

GENE. Dad?

TOM. Mm? Margaret? *(Coming to a little more and looking up at Gene.)* . . . Oh, Gene . . . I must have dozed off.

GENE. Alice is here.

TOM. Alice? . . . What for? *(He is genuinely confused.)*

ALICE. *(Comes from the shadows.)* Hello, Dad.

TOM. *(Looks around, a bit panicky, confused . . . then he remembers.)* Oh. . . . Oh, yes. *(He bites his upper lip, and with his gnarled hands grips theirs for a moment of affection and family strength. Alice kisses him on the cheek. . . . As the lights dim on the "Home" area, they come up on a "Graveyard" area. Tom, Gene and Alice and all the people we have met, are gathering as Dr. Pell starts his eulogy.)*

DR. PELL. Margaret Garrison was a loving wife and a kind and generous Mother, and a public spirited member of the community. The many people who were touched by her goodness can attest to the pleasure and joy she brought them through her love of life and her power to communicate this love to others. . . . The many children, now grown . . .

GENE. *(Turns from the family group.)* Only a dozen or so people were at my Mother's funeral. Most of her friends were dead, or had moved to other cities, or just couldn't make it. Fifteen years earlier, the church would have been filled. There were a few men sent from Rotary, a few women from the Garden Club, the Mother's Club, the Woman's Club, and a few of the members of her bridge club were there. . . . The hundreds of children who had listened to her tell stories year after year on Christmas Eve, were all gone, or had forgotten. . . . Perhaps some of them who were still in the neighborhood looked up from their evening papers to say, "I see Mrs. Garrison died. She was nice. . . . Well, she was an old lady. . . ." *(He turns to rejoin the family group.)*

DR. PELL. Earth to earth . . . ashes to ashes . . . dust to dust. . . . The Lord giveth and the Lord taketh away. . . . Blessed be the name of the Lord. . . . Amen. *(Tom comes to shake hands with*

Dr. Pell. *The others drift about, exchanging nods and gradually leave, during the following . . .)*

TOM. Well, it's a nice place up here.

GENE. *(Who has wandered over to look at another grave.)* Yes.

TOM. Your Mother and I bought it soon after we were married. She thought it a strange thing to do, but we bought it. *(He looks at grave Gene is looking at.)* Now, let's see, that's . . .

GENE. Carol.

TOM. Who?

GENE. Carol. My wife.

TOM. Oh, yes. *(He reaches out a sympathetic hand towards Gene . . . then moves away . . .)* There's room for three more burials up here, as I remember. There . . . there . . . and there. I'm to go there, when the time comes. *(He looks around for a moment.)* This plot is in terrible shape . . . I paid three hundred dollars some years ago for perpetual care, and now look at it. Just disgraceful . . . I'm going to talk to that Superintendent. *(And he strides off. . . . The lights change. . . . Alice and Gene move into another area, what might be a garden with a bench. . . . For a moment, neither says anything. Gene lights a cigarette and sits on the grass.)*

ALICE. I don't know how you feel, but I'd like to figure out some kind of memorial for Mother. . . . Use some of the money she left.

GENE. Yes, definitely.

ALICE. Maybe some shelves of books for the Children's Library. Christmas books with the stories she liked to tell.

GENE. That's a good idea. *(There is a long and awkward pause.)*

ALICE. Well, Gene . . . what are we going to do?

GENE. *(Frowns.)* Mother always said put her in an old people's home. She had one all picked out.

ALICE. Sidney's Mother and Father saw it coming and arranged to be in one of those cottage colonies for old people.

GENE. Mother and Dad didn't.

ALICE. I think you should go ahead and get married and move to California. . . . But . . . I might as well get this off my chest, it would be murder if he came to live with us. In the first place, he wouldn't do it, feeling as he does about Sid, and the kids can't stand how he tells them how to do everything.

GENE. I think you're right. That would never work. *(There is a pause. Gene looks out at the garden.*) I can't tell you what it does to me as a man . . . to see someone like that . . . a man who was distinguished, remarkable . . . just become a nuisance.

ALICE. (*Is disturbed at what her brother may be thinking.*) I know I sound hard, but he's had his life . . . and as long as we can be assured that he's taken care of. . . . Oh, I'll feel some guilt, and you, maybe more. But my responsibility is to my husband and my children.

GENE. Yes. That's *your* responsibility.

ALICE. And your responsibility is to yourself . . . to get married again, to get away from memories of Carol . . . and her whole world. Have you called California?

GENE. (*Frowns.*) No.

ALICE. If I were the girl you were planning to marry, and you didn't call me to tell me your Mother had died . . .

GENE. (*Gets up . . . disturbed . . .*) I just haven't wanted to go into it all with her . . .

ALICE. (*Understanding . . . but worried.*) Gene, my friend . . . my brother. . . . Get out of here!

GENE. Look, Alice . . . your situation is quite different. Mine is very complex. You fortunately see things very clearly, but it's not so easy for me . . . (*Alice looks at Gene, troubled by what his thinking seems to be leading to. After a moment . . . reflective.*) We always remember the terrible things about Dad. I've been trying to remember some of the others. . . . How much he *did* do for us.

ALICE. I'm doing a lot for my kids. I don't expect them to pay me back at the other end. (*Gene wanders around, thinking, scuffing the grass.*) I'm sure we could find a full-time housekeeper. He can afford it.

GENE. He'd never agree.

ALICE. It's that or finding a Home. (*Gene frowns.*) Sidney's folks like where they are. Also, we might as well face it, his mind's going. Sooner or later we'll have to think about Powers of Attorney, perhaps committing him to an Institution.

GENE. God, it's all so ugly.

ALICE. (*Smiling.*) Yes, my gentle Gene . . . a lot of life is.

GENE. Now, look, don't go trying to make me out some softhearted . . . (*He can't find the word.*) I know life is ugly.

ALICE. Yes, I think you know it. You've lived through a great deal of ugliness. But you work like a Trojan to deny it, to make it not so. (*After a moment . . . not arguing.*) He kicked me out. He said he never wanted to see me again. He broke Mother's heart over that for years. He was mean . . . unloving. . . . He beat the Hell out of you when you were a kid. . . . You've hated and feared him all your adult life . . .

GENE. (*Cutting in.*) Still he's my Father, and a man. And what's happening to him appalls me as a man.

ALICE. We have a practical problem here.

GENE. It's not as simple as all that.

ALICE. To me it is. I don't understand this mystical haze you're casting over it. I'm going to talk to him tomorrow, after the session with the lawyer, about a housekeeper. (*Gene reacts but says nothing.*) Just let me handle it. He can visit us, and we can take turns coming to visit him. Now, I'll do the dirty work. Only when he turns to you, don't give in.

GENE. I can't tell you how ashamed I feel . . . not to say with open arms, "Poppa, come live with me . . . I love you, Poppa, and I want to take care of you." . . . I need to love him. I've always wanted to love him. (*He drops his arms and wanders off. Alice watches her brother drift off into the garden as: The lights go down in that area. Lights come up in living room area. Tom is seated in his chair . . . writing. . . . Alice comes into the room. Small packing boxes grouped around.*)

ALICE. How are you coming?

TOM. Oh, Alice, I've written out receipts for you to sign for the jewelry your mother left you. . . . And if you'll sign for the things she left the children.

ALICE. All right. (*Signs. Gene comes into the room carrying a box full of his Mother's things.—He exchanges a look with Alice, knowing the time has come for the discussion.*)

TOM. It may not be necessary, but as Executor, I'll be held responsible for these things.

ALICE. Dad, I'd like to talk a little . . . with you . . . about—

TOM. Yes, all right. But first, I'd like to read you this letter I've written to Harry Hall. . . . He and I used to play golf out in New Jersey. . . . He wrote a very nice letter to me about your Mother . . . and I've written him as follows. . . . It will only take a minute. . . . If I can read my own shorthand. . . . (*He adjusts his glasses.*) Dear Harry. . . . How thoughtful of you to

47

write me on the occasion of Margaret's death. It was quite a blow. As you know, she was my inspiration, and had been ever since that day fifty-five years ago when I met her . . . when the clouds hung low and dark for me. At that time I was supporting my younger brother and my sister, and my aged grandfather in a two room flat . . . going to work every day in a lumber mill. Providence, which has always guided me, prompted me to take a night course in shorthand and typing, and also prompted me to go to the Underwood Typewriting Company seeking a position as stenographer. They sent me, God be praised, to the office of T. J. Parks . . . and a job that started at five dollars a week, ended in 1929 when I retired, at fifty thousand a year. . . . That's as far as I've gotten at the moment. (*He looks up for approval.*)

GENE. Dad, I don't think financial matters are particularly appropriate in answering a letter of condolence.

TOM. Oh? (*He looks at letter.*) But it's true. You see, it follows. I'm saying "she was my inspiration" . . . and it seems entirely appropriate to explain that.

GENE. Well, it's your letter, Dad.

TOM. (*Looks it over.*) Well . . .

ALICE. Dad, I'm leaving tomorrow . . . and . . .

TOM. (*Looking up.*) What?

ALICE. I'm going home tomorrow.

TOM. (*Formal.*) Well, Alice, I'm grateful you came. I know it was difficult for you . . . leaving home. Your Mother would have appreciated it. She was very fond of you, Alice.

ALICE. I think we ought to talk over, maybe, what your plans are.

TOM. My plans? I have many letters to answer, and a whole mess in my files and accounts. If the Income Tax people ever asked me to produce my books . . .

GENE. They're not likely to, Dad. Your income is no longer of that size.

TOM. (*A twinkle in his eye.*) Don't be too sure.

ALICE. I didn't mean exactly that kind of plans. I meant . . . Well, you haven't been well.

TOM. (*Belligerent.*) Who said so?

ALICE. Mother was worried to death about— (*Stops.*)

TOM. I was under a strain. Your Mother's health . . . never

knowing when it might happen. Trying to get her to take care of herself, to take it easy. You know the doctor said if she didn't eat more slowly, this might happen.

ALICE. You plan to keep the house?

TOM. Oh, yes. All my things are here. . . . It's a . . . It's a . . . I'll be back on my feet, and my . . . (*Points to his head.*) will clear up. Now this strain is over, I'm confident I'll be in shape any day now.

ALICE. I worry, leaving you in this house . . . alone, Dad.

TOM. (*Looks around . . . very alert . . . defensively.*) I'm perfectly all right. Now don't worry about me . . . either of you. Why, for the last year, since your Mother's first attack, I've been getting the breakfast, making the beds, using a dust-rag. . . . (*He makes quite a performance of this . . . it is a gallant struggle.*) And the laundress comes in once a week and cleans up for me. . . . And Gene here . . . if Gene will keep an eye on me, drop in once or twice a week . . .

ALICE. That's the point.

GENE. (*Low.*) Alice!

ALICE. We think you should have a full-time housekeeper, Dad. . . . To live here.

TOM. (*Trying to kid it off . . . but angry.*) Alone here with me? . . . That wouldn't be very proper, would it?

ALICE. (*Smiling.*) Nevertheless . . .

TOM. No. Now that's final.

ALICE. Dad, Gene and I would feel a lot better about it if—

TOM. —Look, you don't have to worry about me.

ALICE. Dad, you're forgetting things more and more.

TOM. Who says so?

ALICE. Mother wrote me, and—

TOM. —I was under a strain. I just finished telling you. Look, Alice, you can go, leave with a clear mind. I'm all right. (*Gene is touched and moved by his Father's effort . . . his desperate effort to maintain his dignity, his standing as a functioning man.*) Of course, I will appreciate Gene's dropping in. But I'm all right.

ALICE. We still would like to get a full time housekeeper.

TOM. (*Bristling.*) What do you mean, "you would get?" I've hired and fired thousands of people in my day. I don't need anyone *getting* someone for me.

ALICE. Will you do it yourself, then?

49

TOM. No. I told you, No! (*He gets very angry. His voice sharpens and hardens.*) Since I was eight years old I've taken care of myself. What do you two know about it? You were given everything on a platter. At an age when you two were swinging on that tree out there, breaking the branches, I was selling newspapers five hours a day, and at night dancing a jig in saloons for pennies. . . . And you're trying to tell me I can't take care of myself. . . . If I want a housekeeper, and I don't, I'll hire one. . . . I've hired and fired thousands of people in my time. When I was Vice-President of Colonial Brass at fifty thousand a year. . . . Two thousand people. And you tell me I'm incompetent . . . to hire a housekeeper. And how many people have you hired? (*To Gene.*) You teach. . . . Well, all right. That's your business, if that's what you want to do. But don't talk to me about hiring and firing. (*The children are saddened and perhaps a little cowed by this naked outburst . . . the defense of a man who knows that he is slipping, and an angry outburst of hatred and jealousy for his own children. Everyone is quiet for a moment . . . then . . .*)

ALICE. Dad, you might fall down.

TOM. Why fall down? There's nothing wrong with my balance. (*Gene is sick at this gradual attempt to bring to a man's consciousness the awareness that he is finished.*)

ALICE. Sometimes, when you get up, you're dizzy.

TOM. Nonsense. (*He gets up abruptly. He makes great effort and stands for a moment, then one foot moves slightly to steady his balance . . . and the children both look away.*) Now, I appreciate your concern. . . . (*Very fatherly.*) But I'm perfectly able to carry on by myself. As I said, with Gene's help from time to time. . . . I imagine we could have dinner every once in a while, couldn't we, Gene. . . . Once a week or so. Take you up to Rotary. Some of the speakers are quite amusing. (*Alice looks at Gene to see if he is going to speak up.*)

GENE. Sure, Dad.

TOM. Give us some time together at last . . . get to know each other.

ALICE. (*Quietly but firmly.*) Gene wants to get married.

GENE. Alice!

TOM. What?

ALICE. Gene wants to move to California and get married.

50

GENE. Alice, shut up.

ALICE. (*Almost in tears.*) I can't help it. You've never faced up to him. You'd let him ruin your life.

GENE. (*Angry.*) I can take care of my own life.

ALICE. You can't!

TOM. (*Loud.*) Children! . . . Children! (*They stop arguing, and turn to their Father at his command. A note of sarcasm.*) I have no desire to interfere with either of your lives. I took care of myself at eight. I can take care of myself at eighty. I have never wanted to be a burden to my children.

GENE. I'm going to hang around, Dad.

TOM. There's no need to.

GENE. I'll move in here at least till you're feeling better. (*Alice turns away, angry and despairing.*)

TOM. (*Sarcasm.*) I don't want to ruin your life.

GENE. (*Angry now at his Father.*) I didn't say that.

TOM. I have long gotten the impression that my only function in this family is to supply the money to—

GENE. (*Anguished.*) —Dad!

TOM. —To supply the funds for your education, for your—

GENE. —Dad, stop it! (*Tom staggers a little . . . dizzy. Gene goes to his side to steady him. . . . Tom breathes heavily in and out in rage. . . . The rage of this man is a terrible thing to see, old as he is. . . . He finally gets some control of himself.*)

TOM. As far as I am concerned, this conversation is ended. Alice, we've gotten along very well for some years now without your attention.

GENE. (*Protesting . . . but hating the fight.*) Dad.

ALICE. You sent me away. Don't forget that.

TOM. You chose to lead your own life. Well, we won't keep you now.

GENE. Dad . . .

TOM. (*Rage again . . .*) I was competent to go into the city year after year to earn money for your clothes, your food, the roof over your head. Am I now incompetent? Is that what you're trying to tell me? (*He looks at Alice with a terrible look. . . . He breathes heavily for a moment or two . . . and then shaking his head . . . he turns away from both of them and leaves . . . disappearing into the shadows . . .*)

GENE. (*Angry . . . troubled.*) For God's sake, Alice . . .

ALICE. I'm only trying to get a practical matter accomplished . . .

GENE. You don't have to destroy him in the process.

ALICE. I wasn't discussing his competence. . . . Although that will be a matter for discussion soon.

GENE. Look, Alice, just leave it . . . now . . . the way it is. Don't say any more.

ALICE. With you staying on.

GENE. Yes. You can go with a clear conscience.

ALICE. My conscience is clear.

GENE. I am doing this because I want to.

ALICE. You're doing it because you can't help yourself.

GENE. Look, when I want to be analyzed, I'll pay for it.

ALICE. (*Pleading.*) But I saw you. Didn't you see yourself there . . . when he started to rage. Didn't you feel yourself pull in? You shrank.

GENE. I shrank at the ugliness of what was happening.

ALICE. You're staying because you can't stand his wrath. The day you say, "Dad, I'm leaving." . . . You've never been able to stand up to his anger. He's cowed you.

GENE. Look, Alice . . .

ALICE. He'll call you ungrateful . . . and you'll believe him. He'll lash out at you with his sarcasm, and that will kill this lovely, necessary image you have of yourself as the good son. . . . Can't you see that?

GENE. (*Lashing out.*) What do you want us to do? Shall we get out a White Paper? Let it be known that we . . . Alice and Gene, have done all that we can do to make this old man happy in his old age . . . without inconveniencing ourselves, of course. . . . And he has refused our help. So, if he falls and hits his head and lies there until he rots, it is not our fault. . . . Is that it?

ALICE. You insist on—

GENE. (*Running on.*) —Haven't you learned on the couch that people do *not* always do what you want them to do. . . . It is sometimes *we* who have to make the adjustments?

ALICE. The difference between us is that I accept the inevitable sadness of this world without an acute sense of personal guilt. You don't. I don't think anyone expects either of us to ruin our lives for an unreasonable old man.

GENE. It's not going to ruin my life.

ALICE. It is.

GENE. A few weeks . . . a month.

ALICE. Forever!

GENE. Alice, let's not go on discussing it. I know what I am going to do. Maybe I can't explain my reasons to you. I just know I can't do anything else. Maybe there isn't the same thing between a Mother and a Daughter . . . but the "old man" in me feels something very deep . . . wants to extend some kind of mercy to that old man. . . . And . . . I never had a Father . . . I ran away from him. . . . He ran away from me. . Maybe he's right. Maybe it is time we found each other.

ALICE. I find that sentimental crap! . . . I think this is all rationalization to make tolerable a compulsion you have to stay here. You hate the compulsion, so you've dressed it up to look nice.

GENE. How do you know what you're saying isn't a rationalization to cover up a callousness, a selfishness, a coldness in yourself? To make it smell nice?

ALICE. What do you think you'll find?

GENE. I don't know.

ALICE. You hope to find love. Couldn't you tell from what he just said what you're going to find? Don't you understand he's got to hate you? He may not think it in his head or feel it in his heart, but you are his enemy! From the moment you were born a boy, you were a threat to this man and his enemy.

GENE. That sounds like the textbooks, Alice.

ALICE. He wants your balls . . . and he's had them! (*Gene stands . . . starts to leave the room.*) I'm sorry. I want to shock you. When has he ever regarded you as a man, an equal, a male? When you were a Marine. And that you did for him. Because even back there you were looking for his love. You didn't want to be a Marine. "Now, Poppa, will you love me?" And he did. No, not love. But he was proud and grateful because you gave him an extension of himself he could boast about, with his phoney set of values. . . . When was he ever proud about the thing *you* do? The things *you* value? When did he ever mention your teaching or your books, except in scorn?

GENE. You don't seem to have felt the absence of a Father. But I

53

feel incomplete . . . deprived . . . I just do not want to let my Father die a stranger to me.

ALICE. You're looking for something that isn't there, Gene. . . . You're looking for a Mother's love in a Father. . . . Mothers are soft and yielding. Fathers are hard and rough, and to teach us the way of the world, which is rough, which is mean, which is selfish and prejudiced.

GENE. All right. That's your definition. And because of what he did to you, you're entitled to it.

ALICE. I've always been grateful to him for what he did. He taught me a marvelous lesson, and has made me able to face a lot . . . and there has been a lot to face, and I'm grateful as Hell to him. Because if I couldn't get the understanding and compassion from a Father, who could I expect it from, in the world? Who in the world, if not from a Father? So I learned, and didn't expect it, and I've found very little, and so I'm grateful to him. I'm grateful as Hell to him. (*The growing intensity ends in tears, and she turns her head.*)

GENE. (*Looks in pity at the involuntary revelation of her true feeling. . . . He moves to her and touches her.*) I'll stay, Alice . . . for a while, at least . . . for whatever reasons. Let's not argue any more.

ALICE. And Peggy?

GENE. She'll be coming in a week or two, we'll see.

ALICE. Don't lose her, Gene. Maybe I'm still fouled up on myself, but I think I've spoken near the truth about you.

GENE. I keep wondering why I haven't called her . . . or wanted to call her. Why I seem so much closer to Carol at the moment.

ALICE. (*Gently . . . tentatively.*) The image . . . of the eternally bereaved husband . . . forgive me . . . the dutiful son. . . . They're very appealing and seductive. . . . But they're not living. (*Gene just stands, looking at her, thinking about what she has said. Alice kisses him on the cheek . . .*) Good night, Gene.

GENE. (*His hands on her shoulders . . .*) Good night.

ALICE. (*She suddenly puts her head tight against his shoulder and holds him . . .*) Suddenly I miss Mother so . . . (*She sobs. . . . He just holds her and strokes her back.*)

GENE. Yes. (*And he holds her, comforting her . . . as the lights dim. . . . After a few moments of darkness, the lights come up*

54

on *Tom* . . . *in his bedroom* . . . *in pajamas and bathrobe* . . . *kneeling by his bed* . . . *praying.* . . . *On his bed is a small top drawer of a bureau, filled with mementoes. Gene comes in.* . . . *He stands in the shadows and watches his Father at his prayers.* . . . *Gene does not pray any more* . . . *and he has always been touched by the sight of his Father praying.* . . . *Tom gets up and starts to untie his bathrobe.* . . . *Gene enters* . . .) You ready to be tucked in?

TOM. (*Smiling.*) Yes. . . . (*Loosening his robe.*) Look at the weight I've lost.

GENE. (*Troubled at the emaciated body* . . . *which is pathetic.* . . . *The face is ruddy and strong* . . . *the body* . . . *an old man* . . .) Since when?

TOM. Oh, I don't know.

GENE. (*Tapping his Dad's stomach.*) Well, you had quite a little pot there, Dad.

TOM. (*Smiling.*) Did I?

GENE. Yes.

TOM. But look . . . all through here, through my chest.

GENE. Well, we'll put some back on you. You've been eating preety well this last week.

TOM. (*Looking at his own chest.*) You know, I never had hair on my chest. . . . I don't understand it. . . . You have hair on your chest . . . I just didn't have any. . . . Well . . . I'm confident if I could get some exercise. . . . Do you remember when I used to get you up in the morning . . . and we'd go down and do calisthenics to the radio?

GENE. (*Smiling.*) Yes.

TOM. (*Stands very straight* . . . *swings his arms* . . .) One-two-three-four . . . one-two-three-four . . .

GENE. Hey, take it easy.

TOM. I used to swing the Indian Clubs every day at lunch-time . . . I gave you a set once, didn't I?

GENE. I think so.

TOM. We'll have to dig them out. (*Starts bending exercises.*) One-two-three-four . . . one-two-three-four.

GENE. Why don't you wait till morning for that?

TOM. Remember when we used to put on the gloves and spar . . . down on the side porch? . . . I don't think you ever liked it very much. (*He crouches in boxing position.*) The manly art of self-defense . . . Gentleman Jim Corbett. . . . Now it's something else again. . . . Oh, well, things to worry about. . . . But I intend to get over to the Club . . . play some golf, sit around and swap stories with the boys. . . . Too bad you never took up golf. . . . Alice could have played a good game of golf. . . . But she had a temper. . . . Inherited it from your Mother's Father. . . . Irascible old bastard, if you'll pardon my French. (*He fishes in the bureau drawer.*) I was looking through my bureau drawer . . . I don't know, just going over things. . . . Did you ever see this? (*He takes out a small revolver.*)

GENE. Yes.

TOM. Never had occasion to use it. Oh, I took it out West one Winter when we went to Arizona instead of Florida. . . . Shot at rattlesnakes in a rock pile. (*Take pot shots.*) I don't have a permit for this any more. . . . (*Starts putting it back in box.*) I suppose they wouldn't give me one. I don't know anyone up there any more. When I was Mayor, cops on every corner would wave . . . "Hello, Mr. Garrison . . . 'Morning, Mr. Garrison." Now, one of the young whipper-snappers gave me a ticket, just before we left for Florida. Said I'd passed a full-stop sign. That's what *he* said. . . . First ticket I had in forty or more years of driving . . . so keep this quiet. (*He takes out a packet of photographs wrapped in tissue paper.*) Pictures . . . I think you've seen most of them. . . . The family.

GENE. (*Very tentatively.*) You know, Dad, I've never seen a picture of your Father. (*Tom looks at him a long time . . . should I really show him . . . then finally, with his hatred showing on his face, he unwraps another tissue and hands over a small picture. . . . Looks at it a long moment.*) He's just a boy?

TOM. That was taken about the time he was married.

GENE. I'd always thought of him as . . . the way you talked about him . . . as . . . (*Gene is obviously touched by the picture.*)

TOM. Oh, he was a fine looking man before he started to drink. Big, square, high color. . . . But he became my mortal enemy. . . . Did I ever show you that? (*He takes out a small piece of paper.*) Careful. . . . When I set up a home for my brother and sister . . . one day we were all out, and he came around . . . and ripped up all my sister's clothes and shoes. . . . Drunk, of course. . . . A few days later he came around to apologize and ask for some money, and I threw him out. . . . The next day he left this note . . . "You are welcome to your burden."

GENE. And you kept it?

TOM. Yes. I never saw him again until many years later he was dying . . . in Bellevue . . . and someone got word to me, and I went down and asked him if he wanted anything. . . . He said he'd like some fruit . . . so I sent him in a few oranges. He died the next day.

GENE. There must have been something there to love . . . to understand.

TOM. In my Father? . . . (*Shakes his head . . . "No." Shows Gene another card.*) Do you remember this? . . . (*Reads.*) "To the Best Dad in the World on Father's Day." . . . That was in . . . (*Turns over and reads notation.*) 1946. . . . Yes. (*Emotional.*) I appreciate that, Gene. That's a lovely tribute . . . I think I have all your Father's Day cards here. . . . You know your Mother used to talk of you children as her jewels. . . . Maybe because my interests were different, I've always said you were my dividends. . . . You know . . . I didn't want children. . . . Coming from the background I did . . . and we didn't have Alice for a long time. . . . But your Mother finally persuaded me. . . . She said they would be a comfort in our old age. . . . And you are, Gene . . .

GENE. (*Touched . . . but embarrassed . . . and uncomfortable . . .*) Well . . .

TOM. (*Fishes in the drawer, and brings out a sheet of paper.*) A program of yours from college . . . some Glee Club Concert . . . I've got everything but the kitchen stove in here. . . . (*Looks over the program.*) Do you still sing?

GENE. (*Smiling.*) Not in years.

TOM. That's too bad. You had a good voice. But we can't do everything . . . I remember your mother would sit at the piano, hour after hour, and I'd be up here at my desk, and I'd hear you singing . . .

GENE. (*Smiles . . . kidding.*) You always wanted me to sing "When I Grow Too Old To Dream."

TOM. Did I? . . . I don't remember your ever singing that. . . You always seemed to be just finishing when I came into the room. . . . (*Looks at Gene.*) Did you used to sing that for me?

57

GENE. (*Not a joke any more.*) No. . . . But you always asked me to sing it for you.

TOM. Oh. . . . (*Puts the program away . . .*) Well, I enjoyed sitting up here and listening. (*He pokes around in his box . . . and takes something out . . . in tissue paper. Unwraps a picture . . . carefully.*) And that's my Mother.

GENE. (*Gently.*) Yes. I've seen that, Dad. It's lovely.

TOM. She was twenty-five when that was taken. She died the next year. . . . I carried it in my wallet for years. . . . And then I felt I was wearing it out. So I put it away. . . . Just a little bit of a thing. . . . Barely so high. . . . (*He starts to cry . . . and the deep, deep sobs finally come and his emaciated body is wracked by them . . . it is a terrible, almost soundless sobbing. . . . Gene comes to his Father and puts his arms around him and holds him. . . . After a few moments . . .*) I didn't think it would be this way . . . I always thought I'd go first. (*He sobs again . . . gasping for air . . . Gene continues to hold him . . . inevitably moved and touched by this genuine suffering . . . Finally . . . gets a stern grip on himself.*) I'm sorry . . . (*Tries to shake it off.*) It just comes over me. . . . It'll pass. . . . I'll get a hold of myself.

GENE. Don't try, Dad. . . . Believe me, it's best . . .

TOM. (*Angry with himself.*) No. . . . It's just that. . . . I'll be all right. (*He turns and blows his nose.*)

GENE. It's rough, Dad. . . . It's bound to be rough.

TOM. (*Shakes his head to snap out of it . . .*) It'll pass . . . it'll pass . . . (*Starts to wrap up the picture of his Mother.*)

GENE. Can I help you put these things away, Dad?

TOM. No. . . . No. . . . I can. . . . (*He seems to be looking for something he can't find . . .*) Well, if you would. (*Gene helps him wrap the pictures . . .*) I don't know what we'd do without you . . . (*And together they put the things back in the box. . . . As they put the things back in the box, Gene is deeply moved with feelings of tenderness for his Father. . . . After a few moments, he starts, with great consideration.*)

GENE. Dad?

TOM. Yes?

GENE. (*Carefully.*) You remember . . . I wrote you about California . . . and Peggy?

TOM. What?

GENE. The girl . . . in California.

TOM. (*On guard.*) Oh, yes.

GENE. (*Putting it carefully, and slowly.*) I'm thinking very seriously, Dad . . . of going out there . . . to marry . . . and to live. (*Tom straightens up a little.*) Now, I know this is your home, where you're used to. . . . But I'd like you to come out there with me, Dad. . . . It's lovely out there, as you said, and we could find an apartment for you, near us. (*This is the most loving gesture Gene has made to his Father in his life.*)

TOM. (*Thinks for a moment, then looks at Gene with a smile.*) You know, I'd like to make a suggestion. . . . Why don't you all come live here?

GENE. (*Explaining calmly.*) Peggy has a practice out there . . .

TOM. A what?

GENE. She's a doctor. I told you. And children with schools and friends.

TOM. We have a big house here. You always liked this house. It's wonderful for children. You used to play baseball out back, and there's that basketball thing.

GENE. Dad, I'd like to get away from this part of the country for a while. It's been rough here ever since Carol died. It would be good for you too, getting away.

TOM. Your Mother would be very happy to have the house full of children again. I won't be around long, and then it would be all yours.

GENE. That's very kind of you, Dad. But I don't think that would work. Besides her work and the children, all Peggy's family is out there.

TOM. Your family is here.

GENE. Yes, I know.

TOM. Just me, of course.

GENE. You see, the children's Father is out there, and they're very fond of him and see him a lot.

TOM. Divorced?

GENE. Yes.

TOM. You know, Gene, I'm only saying this for your own good, but you went out there very soon after Carol's death, and you were exhausted from her long illness, and well, naturally, very susceptible . . . I was wondering if you've really waited long enough, to know your own mind.

GENE. I know my own mind.

TOM. I mean, taking on another man's children. You know, children are far from the blessing they're supposed to be. . . . And then there's the whole matter of discipline, of keeping them in line. You may rule them with a rod of iron, but if this Father—

GENE. (*Cutting in.*) I happen to love Peggy.

TOM. (*Looks at Gene a long moment.*) Did you mention this business of California to your Mother?

GENE. (*Gets the point, but keeps level.*) She mentioned it to me, and told me to go ahead, with her blessings.

TOM. She would say that, of course. . . . But I warned you.

GENE. (*Turns away.*) For God's sake—

TOM. (*Giving up, angry.*) All right, go ahead. I can manage. . . . (*His sarcasm.*) Send me a Christmas card . . . if you remember.

GENE. (*Enraged.*) Dad!

TOM. What?

GENE. I've asked you to come with me.

TOM. And I've told you I'm not going.

GENE. I understand that, but not this "send me a Christmas card, if you remember."

TOM. I'm very sorry if I offended you. Your Mother always said I mustn't raise my voice to you. (*Suddenly hard and vicious.*) Did you want me to make it easy for you the way your Mother did? Well, I won't. If you want to go, go!

GENE. God damn it. . . .

TOM. (*Running on.*) I've always known it would come to this when your Mother was gone. I was tolerated around this house because I paid the bills and—

GENE. Shut up!

TOM. (*Coming at him.*) —Don't you—

GENE. (*Shouting.*) —Shut up! I asked you to come with me. What do you want? What the Hell do you want? If I lived here the rest of my life, it wouldn't be enough for you. I've tried, God damn it, I've tried to be the dutiful son, to maintain the image of the good son. . . . Commanded into your presence on every conceivable occasion. . . . Easter, Christmas, Birthdays, Thanksgiving. . . . Even that Thanksgiving when Carol was dying, and I was staying with her in the hospital. "We miss you so. Our day is nothing without you. Couldn't you come up for an hour or two after you leave Carol?" You had no regard for what was really going on. . . . My wife was dying!

TOM. Is it so terrible to want to see your own son?

GENE. It is terrible to want to possess him . . . entirely and completely!

TOM. (*Coldly . . . after a moment.*) There will be some papers to sign for your Mother's Estate. Be sure you leave an address with my lawyer. . . .

GENE. (*Cutting in.*) Dad!

TOM. (*Cutting, no self-pity.*) From tonight on, you can consider me dead. (*Turns on him in a rage of resentment.*) I gave you everything. Since I was a snot-nosed kid, I've worked my fingers to the bone. You've had everything and I had nothing. I put a roof over your head, clothes on your back—

GENE. —food on the table.

TOM. —things I never had.

GENE. I know!

TOM. You ungrateful bastard!

GENE. (*Seizes him, almost as though he would hit him.*) What do you want for gratitude? Nothing, nothing would be enough. You have resented everything you ever gave me. The orphan boy in you has resented everything. I'm sorry as Hell about your miserable childhood. When I was a kid, and you told me those stories, I used to go up to my room at night and cry. But there is nothing I can do about it . . . and it does not excuse everything . . . I *am* grateful to you. I also admire you and respect you, and stand in awe of what you have done with your life. I will never be able to touch it. (*Tom looks at him with contempt.*) But it does not make me love you. And I wanted to love you. (*Tom snorts his disbelief.*) You hated your Father. I saw what it did to you. I did not want to hate you.

TOM. I don't care what you feel about me.

GENE. I do. . . . (*He moves away from his Father.*) I came so close to loving you tonight . . . I'd never felt so open to you. You don't know what it cost me to ask you to come with me . . . when I have never been able to sit in a room alone with you. . . . Did you really think your door was always open to me?

TOM. It was not my fault if you never came in.

GENE. (*Starts to move out.*) Goodbye, Dad. I'll arrange for someone to come in.

TOM. (*Shouting.*) I don't want anyone to come in. I can take care of myself. I have always had to take care of myself. Who needs you? Out! . . . I have lived each day of my life so that I could look any man in the eye and tell him to GO TO HELL! (*This last, wildly at Gene. The lights dim out quickly, except for a lingering light on Gene. . . .*)

GENE. (*After a few moments.*) That night I left my Father's house forever . . . I took the first right and the second left . . . and this time I went as far as California. . . .

Peggy and I visited him once or twice . . . and then he came to California to visit us, and had a fever and swollen ankles, and we put him in a hospital, and he never left. . . . The reason we gave, and which he could accept, for not leaving . . . the swollen ankles. But the real reason . . . the arteries were hardening, and he gradually over several years slipped into complete and speechless senility . . . with all his life centered in his burning eyes. (*A Nurse wheels in Tom . . . dressed in a heavy, warm bathrobe . . . and wearing a white linen golf cap . . . to protect his head from drafts. . . . The Nurse withdraws into the shadows . . .*) When I would visit him, and we would sit and look at each other, his eyes would mist over and his nostrils would pinch with emotion. . . . But I never could learn what the emotion was . . . anger . . . or love . . . or regret. . . .

One day, sitting in his wheel chair and staring without comprehension at television . . . he died . . . alone . . . without even an orange in his hand. (*The light fades on Tom . . .*)

Death ends a life . . . but it does not end a relationship, which struggles on in the survivor's mind . . . towards some resolution, which it never finds.

Alice said I would not accept the sadness of the world . . . What did it matter if I never loved him, or if he never loved me? . . . Perhaps she was right. . . . But, still, when I hear the word Father . . . (*He cannot express it . . . there is still the longing, the emotion. . . . He looks around . . . out . . . as though he would finally be able to express it . . . but he can only say . . .*) It matters. (*He turns and walks slowly away, into the shadows . . . as the lights dim. . . .*)

THE END

A NOTE ON THE PRODUCTION

With a few exceptions, the scenes are intended to cross-fade into one another, the lights going down on one area and coming up immediately on another area. There are probably a number of ways to get the few props on and off the stage. The method Jo Mielziner devised for the New York production utilized two revolving "doughnuts" on either side of the stage, which allowed chairs, tables, hospital bed to be set up behind screens, and then revolved into place in front of the screen, and revolved back at the end of the scene. The screens were also used for projections.

PROPERTIES

ACT ONE:

Small hand truck for luggage
    One large suitcase
    One smaller suitcase
    One hat-box
    One make-up case
Large hand truck for luggage
    Ten assorted suitcases including one gray "2-suiter" and one
        smaller smaller gray one to match it
Pullman seat
    Two popular novels
One folding wheel chair
White orchid corsage (for Margaret)
Wicker armchair with cushion
Small wicker stool to match, 18" high
Newspaper—opened at financial page
Pair of gardening gloves—ladies' (for Margaret)
Three cut hyacinths
Pedestal dining table, 36" square
    Table cloth
    4 Schrafft menus
    Sugar bowl with envelopes of sugar
    Salt and pepper shakers, filled
4 dining chairs
Small round tray
    1 vodka martini, with lemon peel
    1 gin martini, with lemon peel
    2 cocktail napkins
Order pad and pencil
Chaise longue
    Afghan
    3 pillows—one of them heart-shaped
Footstool
Small table beside chaise
    Frilly lamp
    Book with handkerchief in it for book-mark
Single straight chair
Large old armchair (for Tom)
    Extra pillow

Small end table beside it
Telephone on table
Portable T.V. on low stand (height 24″ overall)
Newspaper
2 straight "waiting room" chairs
1 small magazine table between them
2 large leather club chairs—matching
1 stemmed wine glass
1 hand bell
1 order pad and pencil
One hospital bed
    Two pillows, with pillow slips
    Two sheets
    One spread
One oxygen tent, folded back at head of bed
One white bedside cabinet
    Large vase of cut flowers
    Magazine for Nurse
Two metal side chairs

Personal:
Watch
Pad and pencil   } (Gene)
Slip of paper
Hearing aid (Margaret)
Diamond ring
Glasses
Cigarettes and matches } (Tom)
Notebook
Watch
Large "name" button (Dr. Pell)

ACT TWO:
Small ladies' suitcase
Large manila envelope
    Small string of pearls
    Wedding ring
Office desk
    Desk blotter
    Note pad
    Fountain pen in stand
    Ash-tray
Armchair
Standing ash-tray

Bar—"banquette"
Small round pedestal table, with cover
Ash-tray
Two highballs
Ladies' smart overnight case
Margaret's will, official-looking, with seals, etc.
Small garden bench, with back and arms
Folding clip-board, with paper
Fountain pen
Two receipts to be signed
Small chest of drawers—18" high
Ottoman—18" high
Sewing basket, filled
Three boxes of memorabilia
    10 or 12 pictures, loose and in frames
    1 jewel box
    1 dried flower corsage
    4 boxes of handkerchiefs, unopened
    Ledgers
    Notebooks
    Cookbooks
    Albums
    A folding fan
    5 pieces of sheet music
15 assorted books in three piles
Handwritten letter
Tom's brass bed
    Pillow in pillow case
    2 sheets
    1 blanket
    1 folded spread
One dresser drawer—18" wide by 4" deep
    1 large manila envelope of photographs
    1 small photograph of Tom's mother, wrapped in tissue paper
    1 small photograph of Tom's father, wrapped in worn newspaper
    1 small revolver
    1 Glee Club program
    1 single Father's Day card
    1 pack of 25 Father's Day cards with rubber band around them
    1 small piece of paper (note)
Wheel chair

Personal:
Cigarette and matches (Gene)

WARDROBE

GENE:

Grey single-breasted suit
Blue neck-tie
White or very light blue shirt
Black shoes
Charcoal-olive raincoat
(No hat)
Blue pullover sweater

TOM:

Dark blue pin-stripe conservative suit with vest, with pocket
    watch and chain
Black shoes
White shirt
Red neck-tie, Act One
Dark neck-tie, Act Two
Black Chesterfield topcoat
Grey felt hat
Dark raincoat
Camel's hair bath-robe
Old brown leather bedroom slippers
Blue cotton pajamas
Dark blue bath-robe

MOTHER:

Lilac wool suit
    Blouse
Bone-colored shoes
Purse
Gloves
Hat
Light filmy stole or scarf
Bed jacket

PORTER:

Conventional "Red-Cap" uniform
Black shoes

WAITRESS:

    Black uniform (Schrafft's)
    Apron
    Black pumps
    Dark blue raincoat
    Dark blue beret
    Gloves

WAITER:

    Bright red jacket
    Black trousers
    Black shoes
    Black bow-tie
    White shirt
    Brown topcoat
    Brown hat

REV. PELL:

    Dark suit
    White shirt
    Conservative tie
    Black shoes
    Black "academic gown" for funeral

NURSE:

    White uniform } dipped "grey"
    White cap
    White shoes and hose
    Tweed topcoat
    Gloves
    Small hat
    Nurses' cape—blue, lined with red silk

DOCTOR:

    Long white doctor's coat—dipped "grey"
    White shirt
    Dark tie
    Dark brown trousers
    Brown shoes
    Dark brown topcoat
    Dark brown felt hat

MARVIN SCOTT:

    Dark suit
    White shirt
    Neutral tie
    Black shoes
    Oxford grey topcoat
    Felt hat

ALICE:

    Navy blue wool one-piece dress
    Navy blue pumps
    Navy blue smart raincoat
    No hat
    Gloves

NEW PLAYS

• **TAKING SIDES by Ronald Harwood.** Based on the true story of one of the world's greatest conductors whose wartime decision to remain in Germany brought him under the scrutiny of a U.S. Army determined to prove him a Nazi. *"A brave, wise and deeply moving play delineating the confrontation between culture, and power, between art and politics, between irresponsible freedom and responsible compromise." --London Sunday Times.* [4M, 3W] ISBN: 0-8222-1566-7

• **MISSING/KISSING by John Patrick Shanley.** Two biting short comedies, MISSING MARISA and KISSING CHRISTINE, by one of America's foremost dramatists and the Academy Award winning author of *Moonstruck*. *" ... Shanley has an unusual talent for situations ... and a sure gift for a kind of inner dialogue in which people talk their hearts as well as their minds...." --N.Y. Post.* MISSING MARISA [2M], KISSING CHRISTINE [1M, 2W] ISBN: 0-8222-1590-X

• **THE SISTERS ROSENSWEIG by Wendy Wasserstein, Pulitzer Prize-winning author of** *The Heidi Chronicles.* Winner of the 1993 Outer Critics Circle Award for Best Broadway Play. A captivating portrait of three disparate sisters reuniting after a lengthy separation on the eldest's 50th birthday. *"The laughter is all but continuous." --New Yorker. "Funny. Observant. A play with wit as well as acumen.... In dealing with social and cultural paradoxes, Ms. Wasserstein is, as always, the most astute of commentators." --N.Y. Times.* [4M, 4W] ISBN: 0-8222-1348-6

• **MASTER CLASS by Terrence McNally. Winner of the 1996 Tony Award for Best Play.** Only a year after winning the Tony Award for *Love! Valour! Compassion!,* Terrence McNally scores again with the most celebrated play of the year, an unforgettable portrait of Maria Callas, our century's greatest opera diva. *"One of the white-hot moments of contemporary theatre. A total triumph." --N.Y. Post. "Blazingly theatrical." -- USA Today.* [3M, 3W] ISBN: 0-8222-1521-7

• **DEALER'S CHOICE by Patrick Marber.** A weekly poker game pits a son addicted to gambling against his own father, who also has a problem but won't admit it. *"... make tracks to DEALER'S CHOICE, Patrick Marber's wonderfully masculine, razor-sharp dissection of poker-as-life.... It's a play that comes out swinging and never lets up -- a witty, wisecracking drama that relentlessly probes the tortured souls of its six very distinctive ... characters. CHOICE is a cutthroat pleasure that you won't want to miss." --Time Out (New York).* [6M] ISBN: 0-8222-1616-7

• **RIFF RAFF by Laurence Fishburne.** RIFF RAFF marks the playwriting debut of one of Hollywood's most exciting and versatile actors. *"Mr. Fishburne is surprisingly and effectively understated, with scalding bubbles of anxiety breaking through the surface of a numbed calm." --N.Y. Times. "Fishburne has a talent and a quality...[he] possesses one of the vital requirements of a playwright -- a good ear for the things people say and the way they say them." --N.Y. Post.* [3M] ISBN: 0-8222-1545-4

DRAMATISTS PLAY SERVICE, INC.
440 Park Avenue South, New York, NY 10016 212-683-8960 Fax 212-213-1539
postmaster@dramatists.com www.dramatists.com